The Mysterious Beyond

A Basic Guide to Studying Religion

Terry C. Muck

Baker Books

A Division of Baker Book House Co.
Grand Rapids, Michigan 49516

© 1993 by Terry C. Muck
Published by Baker Books
a division of Baker Book House Company
P. O. Box 6287, Grand Rapids, Michigan 49516-6287
Printed in the United States of America

Library of Congress Cataloging-in-Publication Data

Muck, Terry C., 1947–
The mysterious beyond : a basic guide to studying religion / Terry C. Muck.
p. cm.
Includes bibliographical references.
ISBN 0–8010–6303-5
1. Religion—Study and teaching. I. Title.
BL41.M83 1993
200'. 7—dc20
   93–2852

For Edmund Perry, my teacher, mentor, friend. You inspired my interest in Buddhist Vinaya studies, modeled excellence in teaching and scholarship, and challenged my thinking about what it means to be a Christian in a religiously plural world.

Contents

Introduction

Becoming a Student of Religion

The aims of this book are twofold: to investigate how to study religion and to show that such a study need not reduce the content of religion nor minimize personal faith and the commitment of religion students and scholars.

It is true that many people consider it absurd to attempt to study religion objectively. Many even think it blasphemous. Those who consider it absurd do so because it is obvious to them that the God of religion is beyond human understanding. To apply the ruler of science to the universe of religion, they say, is like trying to measure mountains with microscopes. Those who consider the objective study of religion blasphemous do so because for them religion is a feeling of the heart, a humble acquiescence of frail human beings before a sovereign God (or gods). To study God is as inappropriate as servants questioning the ways of kings, or slaves imagining themselves freemen.

Yet both of these attitudes toward religious studies are mistaken—understandable, but mistaken. They are wrong precisely because they do not take into account what every good scientist and scholar knows, that a method of study must match itself to its subject matter. Religious feelings cannot be put on microscope slides any more than chemical reactions can be measured by interviewing molecules. Religion is not studied in test tubes. Religious studies can and must take into account the nature of religious feelings and thinking and devise appropriate ways of studying these things—without destroying them. Religion scholars must account for and must allow the transcendence of the gods just as astronomers must allow for the infinity of the universe, the uncapturable beginnings of time, and the limitations of the human ability to "see." Religion can be studied, but only in ways that do justice to it as a unique, some say ultimate, facet of human existence.

Thus, this book. Let me explain a few things about its design. It is a beginning book: supplemental to the much more detailed methodological studies to which it constantly makes reference; short, so that it can be used in a variety of settings to contribute to the study of other texts and subject matters; simple, because it must be readable for beginners and for interested onlookers to the scholarly study of religion; suggestive because, in order to be supplemental, short, and simple, it cannot afford the space to treat in exhaustive detail all the nuances of the issues raised.

It is a beginning book for the beginner, the student taking his or her first course in religion. I use the material in this book primarily with students in my "Introduction to World Religions" class,[1] most of whom are studying religions other than their own for the first time. But I have also used it in my "Introduction to Modern Religions" class, and it could be used in an introductory class to indigenous religions. As I stated, it is designed to be used in conjunction with a larger, content-oriented text. Its aim is to highlight issues of method that will probably occur to students independently as they study the great world religions: Hinduism, Buddhism, Islam, Christianity, and Judaism. Similarities and differences in these great religions with students' own religions often assault their religious consciences, like stormy waves crashing on the beach. And questions come up: What is religion, anyway? Can religions really be so similar? Are they really so different? What kind of people believe these things? Which one of these religions is true?

Make no mistake. The study of religions is high adventure. It can strike fear into the most placid hearts. It is no wonder that some students come into their first religious studies class with a mixture of curiosity, skepticism, and defensiveness. The world's religious landscape is filled with alien ideas, foreign rituals, and challenging prescriptions on how one should live life. The mental dislocation all of this causes can be considerable. No, the study of religion is not for the faint of heart or the tired of faith.

But the study of religion is for the committed. It has become fashionable in some circles to think that in order to be a good scholar of religions one must have at most a tentative commitment to his or her own faith. *Leave commitment, discipline, and authority at the door all ye who dare to enter the room of interreligious understanding* seems to be the attitude. Yet nothing could be further from the truth. If this book does nothing else, I hope it convinces you that not only is strong commitment to the truth of one's own religious convictions not a hindrance to religious studies, it is actually a tremendous advantage. The best students of religion usually believe that their religion is the right and true one. The worst students of religion are the dilettantes willing to try out every religious ideology. In their insecurity and tentativeness they burn up energies meant for the challenges of scholarly exploration, while the religiously secure energetically sally forth on the paths of new knowledge and understanding. You don't have to give up firm commitment to your own faith in order to study religion. In fact, please don't.

A word of warning, however, for those with strong religious beliefs: Although what I said in the last two paragraphs has perhaps made you eager for the adventure, I feel I must not mislead you about the road ahead. The disciplines associated with the scholarly study of religion are among the most difficult to master in all of academia. The subject matter—people's religions, your religion—is emotionally supercharged. The pull toward bias and premature judgment is extraordinarily strong. Many times you will be pulled in several directions at once. The call of faith, the demands of fidelity to the facts, the apparent fantasies of others will all tug so powerfully in different directions that on some days you will not know which way to go. I have come to enjoy the challenges of such a difficult discipline. But . . . a word to the wise.

What This Book Cannot Do—and What It Can Do

This book cannot cover in depth all the issues of how to study religion. The subject is vast, reaching from archaeological and anthropological field studies to psychological examinations of human religious behavior to sociological constructs to philosophical analysis to the relationship of science and religion. Diana Eck, professor of religion at Harvard University, once said that trying to teach an introduction to world religions course can be like trying to cover the entire history of human thought and behavior in twelve weeks. Because of this breadth of subject matter, the writing and discussion of religious studies methodology—that is to study religion—is vast and largely unsettled terrain.

What can be done in these few pages, however, is to raise *the principal issues associated with the study of religion.* I hope to introduce the outlines of those issues and then point you toward appropriate further study if the nuances of the issues interest you.[2] With that in mind, I have tried to include in the endnote listings of authors who deal with the subjects raised. For further reading you can go to them, and they may very well point you to still other resources. The bibliography at the end of the book serves the same function.

This book cannot make you a fully trained religious studies scholar. As has already been mentioned, becoming a religious studies scholar is a difficult task. It takes time. Most serious students, after taking the initial content courses in history, beliefs, and practices of the world's religions and after sampling different methodological approaches to the study of religion, focus their energies on one or two religions and one methodological approach. In other words, they become specialists.[3]

The book can, however, put you on the road to becoming such a scholar. It is designed to introduce you to a wide range of ways of studying religion—historical, phenomenological, psychological, sociological, philosophical—so you can get a feel for the different subfields of the discipline. At the end of each chapter is an exercise designed to introduce a religious studies skill. Each skill is the anchor for a particular kind of religious study. By trying them all, even if on a basic level, you may begin to get a feel for what you would like to specialize in.

But that choice of specialization also needs to take into account the particular religions or geographical area you decide to study. That's why this book is best used as a supplementary text in a content-oriented course, where the facts and figures of specific religions are taught. The reason for this is simple: religious studies methodology must match the kinds of religions studied. Many indigenous religions, for example, have little if any written texts; to study native American religions you need to be skilled in the anthropological techniques of conducting oral interviews and observing ritual and practice. To investigate religions that have elaborate texts, you need to master a different set of methodological skills. This short book will introduce the spectrum to help you decide your interest.

This book cannot make you religious. If you are looking for a religion to believe in, you need to study books that argue for and against various faiths.[4] This book and other religious studies books do not do that. Religious studies is not an exercise in evangelism. Most religious studies scholars recognize that almost all of the world's religions are evangelistic (some say they all are), and most religious studies scholars do not oppose evangelism. But, as scholars, they attempt to study religions as objectively as possible without, in their scholarly roles at least, arguing for or against a religion from the stance of faith.

This point is important for another reason as well. There is a danger in using religious studies to find personal faith. That danger in approaching the discipline with unintegrated beliefs is the potential growth of cynicism. When you study religions, you study them as they appear in the world, warts and all. You study the various religious expressions of ideals, but it quickly becomes apparent that none of the religions have measured up to those ideals all the time. If you are looking for the perfect religion whose adherents have never made a misstep, you will never find it. If you are on a faith search, religious studies can be a disappointment.

If your faith is secure, however, the study of religions can open your eyes to new and undiscovered reaches of your own faith. As you study the faith systems of others, your own faith may be deepened in remarkable ways. This is one of the pleasurable side effects of the scholarly study of religions.

Finally, this book can teach you the importance of studying religion in this day and age. It will demonstrate that all human beings, at all times in history, and in all places in history have been religious. You will realize that religion is a universal aspect of being human.But you will also learn that religions have been and still are being misused in the world. Politicians and demagogues have used these systems to enslave and abuse people. Wars of religion, religious persecution, and anti-religions have been too common a feature of our history. Religions can be a cause of intense conflict, and unless we learn to understand other people's religious beliefs, these abuses seem destined to continue. I hope this book will convince you that studying religion, both your religion and other religions, can be an important force for world harmony. Learning about religion can be the first step toward understanding that will lead us all toward truth.

Part **1**

The Observer

1

What Am I Observing?

When you ask someone, "What does it mean to define something?" a likely answer will be, "It means to tell what something means." I know. I asked fifteen people this question, and thirteen of them gave an answer that had to do with meaning. To define, according to my interviewees, is to isolate meaning.

Definition does have something to do with meaning. For example, when I define the word *wolfram* as "another name for the element tungsten," I know that wolfram is not the result of a crazy experiment in animal *in vitro* fertilization. I know that wolfram is a metal used for the thin filament that glows in the middle of lightbulbs. My definition demonstrates that I know, as precisely as a nonmetallurgist can, what wolfram is.

The best definitions are precise and limiting. They tell exactly what something is so that it is not confused with something else. The best definition of a bat is one that helps distinguish that animal from a mouse or a bird but does not give so much detail (about the one hundred or so varieties of bats, for example) that it becomes unwieldy. The best definitions isolate the essence of something, those features that it shares with nothing else, and that give the meaning of it.

So, what is the meaning or essence of religion, this thing we are going to study? Immediately we run into a problem. As you will see as you read about more and more religious traditions other than your own, the diversity is extraordinary. Many religions believe in a personal God, but many don't. Some believe that "God" is impersonal, a force or energy. Others believe in many gods. Some, like Theravada Buddhism, don't believe in a god at all. So you can't define religion as a belief in God.

This example about belief in God is just one of thousands that could be given illustrating the variety of religions. Religions come in all shapes and sizes. This makes their study fascinating, but also somewhat confusing. Just when you think you have discovered something common to all religions, you discover a religion (or usually two or three) that doesn't have the same "essence" as a part of its belief structure. After some initial reading in the field, many of us have found ourselves reduced to the old canard often used to "define" good art: I don't know how to describe it, but I know it when I see it. One religious scholar, in fact, thinks religion should be identified along these lines: "To define religion is, then, far less important than to possess the ability to recognise it when we come across it."[1]

But, with religion, variety is not the only problem of definition. If it were, we could resort to the techniques of zoologists who are faced with describing millions of kinds of insects. They handle this by grouping the insects into orders with similar characteristics, then families, genera, species, subspecies, and so forth. We could do the same for religion by creating different families of religions according to certain important characteristics. Some scholars have done this, very helpfully.[2]

Nonetheless, those who have find themselves still left with a problem, a problem unique to religion. The problem revolves around the nature of religion. Religions claim some kind of ultimacy. Religions not only describe answers to the ultimate questions of life (Who am I? What am I doing here? Where am I going?), but also prescribe their answers as the right ones. By its very nature religion claims to go beyond the ordinary and the rational. It claims extraterrestrial dimensions, the ET factor, in some form or another. In short, religion claims special status for itself as the final arbiter of existence. As such, religion in one sense goes beyond definition. If we could define it, it would not be ultimate. Remember the characteristic of a good definition? It limits. And religion (or what religion describes) cannot be limited.

Yet it is extremely important that we be able to put some kind of definition on what it is we are doing when we study religion. Not to do so would leave us hopelessly muddled. It would put us in the position of accepting what Eric Sharpe has called the "Humpty-Dumpty Principle."[3] Remember this exchange in Lewis Carroll's *Through the Looking-Glass and What Alice Found There*?

> "There's glory for you!" [said Humpty Dumpty.]
> "I don't know what you mean by 'glory,'" Alice said.
> Humpty Dumpty smiled contemptuously. "Of course you don't—till I tell you. I meant 'there's a nice knock-down argument for you!'"
> "But 'glory' doesn't mean 'a nice knock-down argument,'" Alice objected.
> "When *I* use a word," Humpty Dumpty said in rather a scornful tone, "it means just what I choose it to mean—neither more nor less."
> "The question is," said Alice, "whether you *can* make words mean so many different things."
> "The question is," said Humpty Dumpty, "which is to be master—that's all."
> Alice was too much puzzled to say anything. . . .

Without definitions we too are puzzled. In order to communicate properly with other scholars who are studying religion, we must be able to say clearly what it is we are studying. "Define your terms" is one of the first things we are likely to hear when we get into a discussion with someone about an idea or an experiment.

Definitions are also helpful in limiting the scope of a person's study. Religion is an enormously broad subject. In order to get anywhere at all, we have to study small chunks of it at a time. So we must, provisionally at least, limit the illimitable. Definitions help in this provisional limiting process.

For example, you may say you want to study the religious reasons why people go to church on Sunday morning. You are aware that people go to church for many reasons, some of them not religious—because of political concerns, because it's good for business, because of that beautiful girl or handsome boy who is always there. But you want to focus on the religious reasons. How do you determine those? To do so, you have to define *religious* in terms that will differentiate it from *psychological, economic, political,* and so forth.

So religious studies scholars, despite the difficulty, plunge in and keep trying to define their field. As a religion scholar, you will need to do the same. But, as you might expect, scholars define religion in different ways. To help, we will discuss these different ways under three general categories, remembering that all are valid and that you might want to use different definitions for different studies, depending on the nature of the project. But you must make clear in your own mind and in the minds of those reading your study which definition you are using.[4]

Essential Definitions

Some scholars persist in trying to isolate the identifying meaning in religion, the essence that sets it apart from other human endeavors. Few, though, persist in trying to define its transcendental element, which goes beyond definition. In Christian terms, few try to define God. The focus in most modern essential definitions is on how human beings respond to their sincere belief in the existence of a transcendental, eternal principle that orders everything. Religious studies scholars in general leave this very difficult defining process to the adherents of the different religions themselves—the theologians who define God in terms of attributes and characteristics, the mystics who define Brahman in terms of personal experience, the poets and storytellers who write myths and create word symbols to lead worshipers to Emptiness, and the artists who paint, compose, and sculpt to involve all of the senses in the God-search.

Religious studies scholars focus, instead, on the human side of this search. They choose to define how human beings respond. The essence of religion, many say, is this human response to the Eternal. It is a response unlike any other. It is not the patriotic thrill one gets at a Fourth of July parade. It is not the sense of deep love one has for one's spouse. It is not the parental concern for a child. It is not the fear one has in the face of a powerful erupting volcano or the peace one experiences on a beautiful, isolated lake in the woods or when viewing a magnificent sunset. It is a feeling or belief close to some of these, yet in its own way unique. It is the religious response that defines what is religious.

Different scholars have defined this feeling in different ways. Friedrich Schleiermacher called it the "feeling of absolute dependence."[5] Psychologist William James called it the "feeling of objective presence."[6] To be sure, not all scholars adopting essentialist definitions locate religion in the feelings. Many locate it in the intellect. One of these, Anders Nygren, defined religion as the belief that there is an eternal world.[7]

One of the weaknesses of this approach to defining religion is that it seems to leave the question about the transcendent up to the human being—to us. Several have asked whether that doesn't sell religion short. In other words, if we leave the objective nature of the transcendent out of the picture, can we really get an accurate reading on what religion is?

Further, it seems to some that scholars who have taken this approach often go the next step and question whether the transcendent has any real existence apart from the human response to the idea of the transcendent. While this is not necessarily a criticism of this type of theory per se (particularly if the scholar does not disavow the existence of the transcendent—or even if he or she does), it does, through guilt by association, make the definition unattractive to some for whom the existence of the transcendent, or God, is very important. "Who does this scholar think he (or she) is, by not affirming the existence of God?" they might ask. From a scholarly point of view, however, the question must be limited to whether or not this really does justice to the definition of religion.

One scholar who attempted to overcome the difficulty of the seeming lopsidedness in the emphasis on humanity in these definitions was Rudolf Otto, who wrote *The Idea of the Holy*. Otto located the essence of religion in the juncture of the *mysterium tremendum* (the awe-full mystery) and the human response to that power, the *mysterium fascinans* (the fascination with the mystery).[8] He called this juncture the numinous. Thus both the object (the transcendent) and the subject (humans) are necessary to produce the thing we know as religion, and the object is more than just a human idea. Otto's views have been met with a mixed response from scholars. Because he tries to allow for both the undefinable ultimate and the definable human response, he falls between the camps of the theologians who accept the existence of the ultimate and the scholars who are skeptical of anything that cannot be defined. As a result, Otto gets praise and censure from both sides.

The value of essential definitions is that they really do try to take the full sweep of religion into account and clearly define the field for scholars and practitioners alike. Philosophers of religion, historians of religion, and phenomenologists of religion are particularly fond of such definitions because these scholars tend to be interested in religions as all-encompassing systems.[9]

Also interested in essentialist definitions, although for reasons quite different from those of historians and philosophers, are theologians within individual religions who want to distinguish their religion (the true one) from the other religions that in some important way(s) do not measure up. This, of course, is legitimate; it is one of the ways theologians are distinguished from religious studies scholars.

Family Definitions

Some scholars believe that there is an essence to religion, but don't believe that this essence can be isolated and defined in the normal sense of definitions. Clifford Geertz is one such scholar who sees the problem this way:

> But how are we to isolate the religious perspective at all? Are we not thrown back on the necessity of defining "religion"? . . . Does not all understanding, or anyway all scientific understanding, depend upon an initial isolation, a laboratory preparation, so to speak, of what it is that one is trying to understand? . . . Well, no. One can begin with an assortment of phenomena almost everyone but the professionally contrary will regard as having something vaguely to do with "religion," and seek for that which leads us to think so.[10]

This is very close to the "I know good art when I see it" kind of definition, but with an added step. Once we agree provisionally on what is religious from this intuitive, inductive stance, we then begin to analyze the pieces and see what kinds of categories we can come up with for a definition. At least that is what anthropologists, like Geertz, and sociologists of religion and psychologists of religion do.

Others, who tend toward this type of definition but still hedge against being too limited and precise, even in a definition arrived at inductively, maintain some kind of flexibility. John Hick, in *An Interpretation of Religion*, argues for what he calls a family-resemblance definition.[11] Hick says that definitions that try to isolate a single element as the essence of religion will always be found to be inadequate, because of the variety problem: someone will always find a religion that is the exception to the rule. Yet Hick as a philosopher of religion needs some kind of overall definition to do his systematic work properly. So he borrows the idea of family-resemblance definitions from another philosopher, Ludwig Wittgenstein, who related it to the idea of games:

> [Games] have no common essence. Some are solitary, others competitive; some individual, others team activities; some depend on skill, others on chance; some are capable of being won or lost, others not; some are played for amusement, others for gain; some are played with balls, others with cards, sticks, etc. What makes us apply the name "game" to this wide assortment of activities, ranging from football to chess, and from a solitary child playing with her doll to the Olympic Games, is that each is similar in important respects to some others in the family, though not in all respects to any or in any respect to all.[12]

Hick asks, cannot religions be viewed in the same way? Something holds them all together, but if the definition (the limiting terms) are very precise then some traditions or belief systems that are recognized generally as religions will be eliminated. So let's just view them as all part of a large family that has a rather long list of characteristics allowing each to be a member.

Its flexibility makes this approach to definition very appealing. But it is not without problems. Its principal problem is that it makes determining whether something is a religion or not very difficult. For example, many scholars have argued that Marxism is a religion, even though Marxism is one of the most atheistic opponents of religion in the world. Yet it does satisfy some (not all) of the characteristics of a religion. Its most faithful adherents do use it to answer the ultimate questions of life. It is a total system, including everything about life. On the other hand, it denies the existence of any type of transcendent God. And it rejects reliance on a power outside of humanity. Family-resemblance definitions would not be of much help in deciding whether to include or exclude Marxism as a religion. Most would probably include it because it seems to fit into the general category of systems called religions. But the boundaries would be fuzzy.

I had an experience of this sort several years ago when I was teaching a world religions class at the University of Texas. One of my first lectures was on the definition of religion. After class a student came forward and said, "According to the definition you gave, Alcoholics Anonymous is a religion. I have just gone through the twelve steps successfully, and I'm a witness to its effectiveness. Right now, it's my religion. Do you agree?"

I had given a four-criteria, family-resemblance type of definition of religion, but the criteria were very broad. After considering them from his point of view, I had to admit that, at this time in his life, A. A. was functioning as his religion. According to most essentialist definitions, however, A. A. would not qualify.

Family resemblance definitions are good to use when it does not matter to your study whether specific individual world views are "in or out" of the spectrum of religions—

when what you are looking for is an understanding of a broad category of belief and behavior with little concern for boundaries.

Working Definitions

Sometimes, however, boundaries are important. Sometimes projects need tight definitions of religion, or an aspect of religion, that will allow clearly demarcated lines of work to take place. We mentioned the example of studying the religious reasons why people go to church on Sunday morning. That study could be limited even more. For example, you could study the *personal* religious reasons why someone goes to church on Sunday morning. Such a study of personal religious behavior might be in the province of a psychologist of religion, who for the purposes of such studies might want a tight, behavioral definition, like this one from William James: "[Religion encompasses] the feelings, acts, and experiences of individual men in their solitude, so far as they apprehend themselves to stand in relation to whatever they may consider the divine."[13] Or you might want to study the *group* religious reasons why someone goes to church on Sunday morning. Such a study might be the province of a sociologist of religion, who for the purposes of such studies might want a tight, sociological definition, like Emile Durkheim's: "A religion is a unified system of beliefs and practices relative to sacred things, that is to say, things set apart and forbidden—beliefs and practices which unite into one single moral community called a Church, all who adhere to them."[14]

The important thing to remember about most working definitions is that they don't claim to be comprehensive. They don't claim to cover all of religion. They carve out certain aspects of religion, to be studied using the social scientific techniques of psychology, sociology, anthropology, archaeology, history, literature, and so forth. The results of these studies are then used by the more global theorists of religion to fit into larger patterns of explanation. But while the work is being done, religion is viewed from a relatively narrow perspective. Actually, most definitions of religion used by religious studies scholars today fall into the working-definition category.

Choosing a Definition

Defining religion is not just theory. The practical implications of this for your own work in religious studies can be summarized by four guidelines:

You don't have to write your own. You need to explicitly state the definition of religion you are using on each and every project, but there are many available to choose from in each subdiscipline of the field of religion. In practice you probably will find yourself working on one area of religion for most of your studies, and you will tend to use the same definition over and over. Feel free to use one from the many scholars who have worked in the field. But also feel free to change or modify their definitions as you have need.

Your definition must match your study. There are many right definitions (and a few wrong ones, I suppose). But it is important that you choose one that matches your study. It is frustrating to try to carry out research on a topic but have a definition that doesn't lead you to ask the right questions. If you are interested in studying the individual prayer habits of people in a certain sect, it is not wise to use a sociological definition of prayer that emphasizes group behavior.

It is sometimes difficult to get started on the right track in this kind of research. Defining your terms with help from experienced researchers is a good idea.

Don't impose your definition on the subjects of your study. I suppose this is common sense, but in the field of religion it is always wise to remind yourself that you are dealing with an important and sensitive part of people's lives. It is almost a sure thing that they define their own religion in a way quite different from you as a religious scholar. We will talk more about this in chapter 6, but for now remember that the purpose of your definition is to allow you to carry out your study effectively, nothing more, nothing less. We are not talking about the truth and falsity of religion. We are trying to make our subject matter manageable in size and understandable in concept.

When reading other research in the field of religious studies, make sure you understand the definition of religion the author/researcher is using. This will save you a lot of confusion and help you evaluate the material in a fair way.

EXERCISE

This can be done in a class or a small-group discussion. Lay a common object on the table. (I usually use my watch.) Ask the group members to write a one-paragraph definition of the object. Have group members read their definitions and note the differences. Some will describe physical features only. Others will describe function and use. Other definitions will be evaluative. In a large class, some will probably be metaphorical. Discuss the many different ways in which we define everyday objects, and then indicate how this applies to religion as well.

Brainstorm five possible research projects, and then write or borrow a definition of religion that would fit each project. Try to think of projects diverse enough so that different definitions of religion are required.

2

What Kind of Observer Am I?

I t is sometimes disconcerting for students to see their own religion described in what seem to be coldly analytical terms. For example, when Christians see the New Testament sayings of Jesus described as "amplifications that go beyond his [Jesus's] own words,"[1] something deep inside is jarred. When Muslim students see early stories about Muhammad (called *Hadith*) described as "unreliable material,"[2] they feel that their faith is being challenged.

The reason for this discomfort is simple. Most of us are used to reading material that is unabashedly in favor of our own religion. We usually read articles and books that assume the truth of Christianity or Islam or Judaism or whatever our religion might be. Often the writers are even promoting the truth of our religion. It is common for the majority of our religious reading to fall into this category.

So when we read something that does not assume the truth of our religion, like the textbooks in a world religions class, warning bells are triggered. What's going on here? we ask ourselves. Is the author saying my religion is not true?

Usually the answer to that question is no. Although some authors do challenge the truth of a religion or religions, that certainly is not the norm in religious studies textbooks. The authors of texts like these are most often deeply religious people in their own right. Their religious commitments are similar to our own. Thus, most world religion texts respect other people's religious beliefs. The last thing most textbook writers want to do is challenge the most deeply held beliefs of others.

But if they are not challenging the truth of our beliefs, what are they doing? The answer is that they are choosing a perspective from which to write. They are taking a stance different from ours in observing religion. Instead of writing as if they were advocates of the religions they are writing about (which would be impossible, considering they are writing about ten to fifteen different religions), they are saying, in effect, "Let's write as if we are sympathetic observers of this religion. We are not opposed to these religions by any means. But let's see what we can learn (and teach) by writing from this different stance."

Actually, there are many different stances scholars take when writing about religion. All are valuable. All add something to our knowledge of religious traditions. None are necessarily threats to the members of any religious community. They are simply different ways of looking at religion.

For example, I have always been fascinated by the weather experts who fly large airplanes into the teeth of a hurricane. Many of us wonder why they do it. Ground-based radar equipment and satellite photos from outer space can track the location, strength, and speed of a developing hurricane very accurately. So why go looking for trouble by adding new (and seemingly dangerous) ways of observation?

The answer is that scientists need as many different stances as possible in order to fully understand this weather phenomenon. Hurricane-hunting airplanes are really sophisticated, flying weather stations. When this equipment is flown into the teeth of 120-mile-per-hour winds, it can take measurements of the hurricane that are otherwise unavailable to other scientists. This information helps predict where the hurricane might go, allowing advance warning to people in its path. Added to the observations from the ground and from outer space, these data give a more fully developed picture of the hurricane—more complete by far than if the risks were not taken.

The same principle applies to observers of religion. The more different looks we can get at a religious tradition, the more accurate and helpful our findings will be, both to members of that tradition and to those who are interested onlookers. The look from a distance is important, but so is the look from inside the whirlwind of religious belief. Generally speaking, a writer about religion can take three main stances: that of the insider, that of the reporter, or that of the specialist.

The Insider

When it comes to our own religion, we are most used to the insider view. This is the stance taken by theologians, pastors, missionaries, and denominational officials. These writers have decided ahead of time that the religion they are writing about is true and correct. They make several assumptions, usually about the nature of God and how God speaks to human beings, and then argue from the implications of those fundamental presuppositions.

For example, a Christian theologian might argue that, since God is our creator and is all-powerful, personal, and interested in each of us, we should act in a way that recognizes our status as a creature trying to return the interest of an all-powerful, infinite being. A Buddhist teacher, on the other hand, might argue that, since the Buddha showed us the perfect way to work ourselves out of our suffering-pervaded existence, we should order our lives in such a way that promotes this escape.

This kind of arguing from broadly accepted principles to the implications of those principles is called deductive thinking. In a deductive study, the facts of the discipline can be increased, but only within the limits of the starting presuppositions. Of course religion can never be a purely deductive affair; the fundamental principles of a faith, from which all else is deduced, have to be arrived at by different means. Usually they are agreed on as the result of a combination of other processes: personal experience of religion, the teachings of an authoritative text such as the Bible, or a supernatural revelation of some other kind.[3] But the emphasis of the insider is agreement on a few general principles and then the logical working out of those principles on the playing field of life.[4]

The truth, of course, is that everyone who writes about religion is an insider of some sort or another. No one comes to the task without some set of basic understandings about religion, whether those views are confessional, experiential, atheistic, or agnostic. But the insider we are talking about here is the one who has consciously made a decision to write about a particular religious tradition from within the understandings of that religion. The kind of writing may vary. It may be an attempt to convert others, it may be an argument about a fine point of theology, or it may be an attempt to describe the system of belief. But the writer makes clear his or her commitment to the truth of the chosen system.

The insider viewpoint is an important one in the study of religion for three reasons. First, only the insider can fully understand one element of religion that differentiates it from philosophy and other world views—the element of ultimate commitment. For example, from the point of view of the believer, at least, religious commitment is different from commitment to the vocation of plumbing. Both of these commitments measure a person's dedication to the task. But the task of plumbing is limited to the way one makes a living; the task of religion answers the deepest questions of life: Who am I? What am I doing here? Where am I going? A serious study of religion demands that this element of commitment be factored into even the academic study of religion as it is in no other academic discipline—simply because this is one of the elements that sets religion apart as a discipline of study.[5] One can study plumbing without studying the commitment of plumbers. Religion cannot be studied without studying the commitment of its adherents, because in large measure commitment is what makes religion unique.

Second, the insider viewpoint gives the student of religion special insight into some of the more difficult areas of belief. In Christianity it is common to call these areas—which deal with such things as the incarnation and the Trinity—the doctrines of mystery. Often the insider can understand these doctrines precisely because of his or her belief. The insider can also illumine us about the way God talks to humanity, which is usually called special revelation and personal experience of God. In short, the very things that are liable to be overlooked or ignored by the outsider are frequently areas of expertise for the insider.

Finally, the insider has a platform from which to look at his or her religion that gives a consistency and authority to the tradition that no others have. John B. Cobb has called this the "essential freedom of the committed."[6] The recognition of the place on which one stands is indispensable to good scholarship and description. Edmund Perry, professor of the history of religions at Northwestern University, told me several times that the best students of religion were the ones who had strong faith commitments of their own. Others, less sure of themselves or striving for some unattainable "objectivity," most often came off as dilettantes, either consciously or unconsciously experimenting with the existential applications of every thought system they came in contact with. Their work tended to be inferior as a result.

Of course, commitment on the part of the insider can be a hindrance to studying religion well. If the motive of the researcher is to present a particular picture of the data no matter what the cost in fidelity to the data or consistency of thought, then the result will be shoddy work. This can be caused by a conscious intent to deceive, or, more often, an unconscious selectivity born of a need to convince. It can be guarded against in two ways. First, the normal peer review of all academic work ought to reveal hidden prejudices and blind spots. Second, the wise insider scholars of religion who are insiders should resolve to clearly articulate their presuppositions to themselves, and to their readers. This allows all those involved to judge for themselves the results of the scholars' work by whatever canons of scholarship they wish to apply.

The important point here is that the insider view need not be seen as a hindrance to good scholarly work in the field of religion. Just the opposite. In fact, if we were limited to only one viewpoint, this one, because of the nature of the discipline, would be the one we should choose.

The Reporter

Fortunately, we do not have to make that choice. Increasing numbers of scholars are deciding to step outside their insider roles, at least temporarily, to look at religion from the stance of a reporter. Somewhat like newspaper reporters, they ask the who, what, when, where, and why questions of religious traditions and of those who hold to those traditions. Sometimes they look at the history of a religion in this way; sometimes they look at the form the religion takes today in all its various churches, temples, mosques, sects, and worship practices. Their goal is always to describe religion in terms that would be acceptable to others interested in "the facts of the case," whether they are members of that religious community or not.

The writers of world religions textbooks are reporters. Their goal is to present the facts of a religious tradition without either advocating that readers follow that religion or discouraging them from doing so. Their primary concern is that readers see, through the textbook description, a religion as it is, including its history, belief structure, practices, and achievements—warts and all. Good news and bad news are included by the reporter, who should be especially careful to avoid making judgments on either.

Most teachers of religion in university religious studies departments are reporters of religion most of the time. This stance matches the need for the scholarly methods adopted by both the hard and the soft sciences. Data gathering without promoting a particular viewpoint is the starting place for academic disciplines.

Interestingly, however, more and more insiders are adopting the stance of reporter for at least part of their work. When insiders like theologians want to bring a new perspective to their thought, a fresh way of looking at old problems, they will sometimes step outside of their role as advocates or systematizers to become collectors of religious data that, at this gathering stage at least, does not have to fit into the preestablished patterns of belief. This change in stance allows the theologian to use the techniques of data gathering and theory formation known as inductive—that is, amassing bits and pieces of information and then building larger theories from those pieces. More and more theologians are using this kind of research to augment and refine their normal deductive procedures.[7] This is particularly effective in the study of certain aspects of religion, such as the history of doctrine, the study of natural revelation, and the understanding of how religious belief affects human beings in everyday life.

The stance of the reporter makes the observer a scientist of religion, if scientist is understood in the sense of the social scientist. The scientist is trying to discover truth, doing his or her best to avoid prejudging the results of experiments. Let the facts determine the outcomes, is the scientist's creed.

Students often have two questions about this approach: First, how does it work? Second, doesn't it mean that my religion becomes dependent on scientists and scholars rather than the Bible or the Vedas (and the other presuppositions insiders work with)? To help answer these two questions, let me relate an example from my own church experience.

Several years ago, a small church I was attending decided it was not reaching the people of the community in which it was located. Most of the people attending the church no longer lived in the neighborhood, and few of the people who moved into the neighborhood chose to join our church. Our congregation wanted to know why.

Two opinions on how to determine the why emerged. Some members of the congregation came to a quick solution based on what they already believed: The newcomers didn't attend because they were not Christian and the spirit of evil was strong among them. In the face of this, they concluded, we must continue to preach the gospel, and God in his own providence and time will bless the church with new members. Others in the congregation wanted to canvass the neighborhood, find out what people wanted in a church, and, if possible, provide that for them. The disagreement between these two groups was sharp.

Both groups provided solid scriptural and theological supports for their positions. Both were well intentioned. In one sense, both were right. Looked at from one way, what they were disagreeing over was the stance they were willing to take in looking at possible solutions to our problem of failure to attract neighbors to our church. The first group was sticking to the insider view, deducing from clear scriptural warrants that we must simply preach the gospel and people will come in God's time. The second group was willing to take the inductive approach—that is, gather some data and from the data devise a strategy.

Does that mean that the second group was allowing the data of social scientific research to dictate church policy? It might. If the survey of neighbors showed that the only way to attract these particular neighbors would be to open a brothel in the church basement and if the church was desperate enough to consider that, then the reporter stance would be dictating policy. But the reporter, as reporter, does not see dictating policy as part of his or her function. Insiders are free to use the data of the reporter as they see fit. They are free to act or not act on it as other considerations dictate. What the reporter does is let the church know as accurately as possible the climate in which the church operates.

The biggest danger of the reporter's stance is not that the function of being a reporter is in itself antithetical to the religions it studies. The previous example should show that it does not need to be. The biggest danger is that reporters often overestimate the purity of their objectivity. Joachim Wach warned against this by suggesting we use the phrase *relative objectivity* when describing the stance of the reporter. Wach was particularly concerned about the historian of religion who adopted the reporter's stance only as a mask for his or her hidden stance of insider (usually of an antireligious variety): "There is something pathetic about the modern historian of religion," he said, "who uses strong words only when he wants to convince us that he has no convictions."[8]

Insiders become dangerous when they use convictions to skew data; reporters become dangerous when they pretend they have no convictions. Only those who articulate their convictions can then temporarily lay them aside to act as faithful, unbiased reporters of the religions they observe.

The Specialist

Many reporters go beyond being general historians of religion or phenomenologists (objective observers of religious phenomena). Many decide to concentrate their studies on one or another aspect of religion, such as religious institutions, religious behavior, or religious philosophy. They often use the methods of study common to sociology, psychology, and philosophy in carrying out their research. Technically, scholars like this are called sociologists of religion, psychologists of religion, and philosophers of religion. Anyone who decides to concentrate on one aspect of religion, however, adopts a specialist stance.

Religion is especially adaptable to this specialist stance, because it covers such a broad spectrum as a discipline. Religion encompasses all of life. It includes how you treat other people (morality) and how you view truth and falsehood, good and evil (ethics). It includes religious behaviors like prayer, church attendance, and worship practices (psychology). It includes church preference, social class, and the role the church plays in society at large (sociology). No one person can hope to understand in detail all these aspects of religion, much less do sophisticated research in each one. Specialization is inevitable and necessary.

Equally inevitable, however, is the danger of overemphasizing this specialization. This danger takes two forms. One stems from the human tendency to view the place where one works as the center of the earth. It is quite common for the specialist to get so deeply into one aspect of religion or one methodology of studying it that the rest of religion pales in significance. Perspective is lost.

The second form is much worse. Scholars of religion have labeled it *reductionism*. The previous distortion is largely unintentional and can be corrected by simply calling attention to other equally important aspects of religious phenomena. Reductionism, on the other hand, is intentional. Put simply, reductionists say that the aspect of religion they choose to study is the only one, and that once religion is explained in psychological, sociological, philosophical, or some other terms, there is nothing more to it. Thus, Sigmund Freud, who claimed religion is nothing more than infantile dependency feelings to be outgrown as humankind matures, was a reductionist. Religion to him was exhausted by the psychological behavior "religious" people displayed.

Unfortunately, religion is particularly susceptible to the reductionist's charge. Any other discipline, challenged to its right to exist as a freestanding department of the academy (or an indispensable feature of life itself), would simply isolate that aspect of its subject matter that clearly defines it and is not covered by any other discipline, and would say, This is it; here we stand.

However, the essential element of religion, as we saw in the last chapter, is not so easily discovered. When all else is stripped away by psychology, philosophy, sociology, and other disciplines, the only thing left is an ultimately undefinable sense of the transcendent and, perhaps, the human response to it. Make no mistake: this is the essence of religion, or what Raffaele Pettazzoni called the "essential character of religion."[9] But it is particularly hard to substantiate this claim because the essence of religion, the transcendent that demands human attention, orders all of existence, and injects meaning into everything else, rises above the scientific categories common to the rest of the curriculum.[10]

One religious scholar, Rudolf Otto, called this ineffable yet essential aspect of religion the Holy. His description of the Holy has received mixed reviews by other scholars of religion, on precisely the grounds one would expect: How do you define the Holy? The answer, of course, is that you don't. Otto himself says in his *Idea of the Holy* (after giving some attempts at description) that if you don't know what he is talking about, don't bother finishing the book.[11] And there you have the difficulties of defining religious studies as a discipline.

In spite of the dangers of the specialist approach, the value of this kind of study is indisputable. A particularly fine example has been the work done by Joseph Campbell on religious mythology.[12] Although Campbell at times seems to come close to overemphasizing myth, he is not a reductionist. By focusing on myth in Eastern and Western religions, by comparing mythological traditions with one another, and by making general readers aware of the beauty and value of these traditions, he has educated us all to the role of "myth" in our religious lives.

Conclusion

As with most divisions of the sort we have just outlined, the separation of stances in real life is not anywhere so neat. Seminary professors who are Christian theologians at times become both reporters and specialists in their approach to religion. University teachers of religion, try as they might to squelch the last vestiges of theological partisanship from their work, will find it squeaking through in subtle ways. Those who relax with that fact and honestly recognize it, will find their work greatly improved. Even the most calloused psychologists of religion will with profit relate their findings to the larger religious spectrum and will be able to do some responsible theologizing with the findings.

In sum, all three stances are important, and this is good. It was an antireligionist who said that "cold gray eyes do not know the value of things." Were his words to be applied to religious studies, he would be speaking deep truth. Deep passion for religion can fire the insider, the reporter, and the specialist almost in equal measure. We must draw on all three sources to find a picture of religion that even begins to do justice to our subject.

In saying this we are not really saying anything startling. It is a common reminder of our human condition to recognize that one viewpoint seldom does the trick in deciding important questions. Most of you will remember how you selected a college to attend. Perhaps you looked through college catalogs and guides for hard numbers on the school and the classes offered. You might have taken a personal visit to the campus for additional objective data. But you also listened closely to the advocates for the school—the admissions officers, students, and faculty members. You knew they were "biased," that they wanted you to come. Still you took that into account and you listened. Perhaps you listened most closely of all to the specialists, the members of the department you wanted to major in. You probably evaluated the information from the various sources differently, but you valued it all. It all helped you find "truth" and see the choices clearly.

There is an objective character of ultimate reality that the student of religion seeks to understand. But it takes data from all three stances, that of the insider, the reporter, and the specialist, to see it clearly.

EXERCISE

One author of a recent text on religion said, "In certain areas of knowledge, . . . personal involvement is not an obstacle to, but a condition of, objectivity."[13] What do you think he meant? Explain your understanding of "objectivity" when it comes to the study of religion. Is objectivity possible?

Write three one-page essays describing a worship service you've attended recently. One of the essays should be written from an insider's stance, one from a reporter's stance, and one from a specialist's stance (for the latter, choose the viewpoint of the psychologist, the sociologist, or the philosopher).

3

What Does It Mean to Take Other Religions Seriously?

Even after we choose a prescribed definition of religion to work with and decide what stance—that of insider, reporter, or specialist—to take, there's still the matter of our attitude toward this whole venture. Attitude doesn't sound like a scientific subject. But I can still remember how important it was to my parents, especially when they would tell me to do a chore. Shoveling snow from our Minnesota sidewalk is an example that comes to mind. I can remember my mother caring a great deal whether I did it with a cheerful, willing attitude or whether I groused the whole time. The same amount of work got done, but for some reason it was important to my mother whether I worked with a good attitude or not. For her, at least, that seemed to affect the whole project.

A similar thing could be said about the scholar of religion—especially the scholar of religion. Because religion is such a visceral topic for all people, subjects and scholars alike, the attitude with which the work is done can not only make it a pleasant or unpleasant task but can actually affect the outcome of the work, perhaps to an extent that pertains in no other academic discipline.

That's a sweeping statement and one hard to defend. Since I think it is true, however, I will try to do so. I will not attack the topic directly, since attitude is not a normal consideration in determining good scientific method. Rather, I will attempt to defend my position by discussing four terms: respect, humility, sensitivity, and advocacy.

Respect

By respect, I mean handling with care the religious beliefs we are working with. Respect means not laughing at, mocking, or belittling the ideas that other people use to order their lives.

This is not always the easiest thing to do. Religious scholars run into some pretty interesting stuff. I'll never forget my initial reaction when I learned that Hindu priests often use cow urine for medicinal purposes. And I know I don't want to know all the details about some of the ingredients that shamans use in their native medicines. It's kind of like not really wanting to know exactly what ingredients go into hot dogs.

Respecting other people's beliefs doesn't mean indiscriminately agreeing with everything you run across. However, it does entail realizing that these sometimes strange beliefs are extremely important to people. Often they are beliefs that have sustained certain groups of people for centuries. That kind of tradition demands respect. As Wilfred Cantwell Smith has noted, "basically, the [religion] student has to deal not with religions, but with religious persons."[1] Persons like you and me.

The question of respect has come up in two hotly debated topics in religious studies in the last one hundred years. One of the two—the universality of religious belief in human beings and cultures—is generally agreed upon by scholars today. There have been no cultures of any significant length or breadth that did without religion for long. Modern totalitarian cultures that deny religion have been unable to do so for extended periods of time. And when such cultures fall (as Marxist cultures in Europe and Asia have recently done), we learn that, in spite of years of consistent persecution and suppression, the indigenous religions have survived, and usually flourished, underground. Religion is a universal human endeavor.

As such religion demands our respect. It appears that people are not religious on a whim. We believe because something about being human drives us to seek a power beyond ourselves that explains and orders existence. And we don't believe things differently from others just to be contrary. Most people choose their religion because it is the religion of their parents and their culture. Just as we wouldn't make fun of someone because of some cultural trait, such as taking one's shoes off at the door of one's house, so civilized people do not belittle religious beliefs just because they are different. In a very important sense, as religious beings we are all in the same boat—searching for a safe harbor.

The second of the two hotly debated issues is a bit more complex. During the late nineteenth and early twentieth centuries, it became common for religious scholars, many of them anthropologists and archaeologists, to attempt to find the common origin of all religion.[2] They did not seek a particular place, like a religious mail-order house that sent out different models of the same basic product, but a common developmental pattern that all religions in all cultures have gone through.[3] The proposed developmental schemes differed. Some located the origin of religion in magic and superstition.[4] Others postulated its origin in "animist" beliefs that all physical things are invested with a spirit: only with time, the theory goes, did these beliefs develop into faith in personal gods and then a single God.[5] Some objected to this scheme and postulated that all religions are grounded in belief in single "high" gods, and that belief in many gods (polytheism) came later.[6] Some, philosophers and psychologists among them, tried to formulate schemes about developing human consciousness that correspond to the different forms religions have taken, usually from generalized communal tribal consciousness to individual consciousness and then, ironically, headed toward a new global consciousness.[7]

This search for developmental schemes was difficult at best. Scientifically, it was difficult because theorists had to rely on a great deal of speculation about the original cultures, which are either gone or changed dramatically. Modern tribal cultures in Africa, Asia, and the South Pacific were studied, and extrapolations were made from those findings to the earliest times. Still, the legitimacy of these searches came to be questioned more and more because of the sheer difficulty of the task of re-creation.

But another problem with these schemes arose, one more in tune with our present subject, respect. It is almost inevitable when talking about development to make the simple associations between new-and-better and old-and-primitive. Books written about primitive, archaic, and superstitious religions were common around the turn of the century, and in many one did not have to scratch far below the surface to reveal a prejudice against the old in favor of the new. Many scholars began to object to these characterizations. Some of the objections had to do the growing unpopularity with evolution as a satisfactory explanation of human consciousness development. Still more criticism arose after World War I, a war that was a blow to those who had optimistically predicted the end of war as human beings became more and more civilized and reached higher and higher planes of consciousness. The net result for religious studies was a renewed emphasis on respect for what had previously been called "primitive" religions. This respect was then extrapolated to include all religions different from one's own.[8] Respect became the attitude of choice for the religious scholar.

The issue remains a difficult one, however. It is complicated by two conflicting observations: First, there does seem to be plenty of evidence to indicate that religions do develop, from simple to complex forms, and often from what seems to be worse to better—from cannibalism to more balanced meals, for example.[9] Second, however, all modern religions have their share of evil in them, and it is difficult sometimes to hold any of them up as models of all we would like to point to as exemplary.

Actually, F. Max Müller, a nineteenth-century scholar who some point to as the founder of the discipline of religious studies, anticipated some of these problems in an essay he wrote in 1885, "The Savage": "I could never understand why a certain hesitation in answering so difficult a question ['Did man begin as a savage?'] should arouse so many angry feelings till it began to dawn on me that those who do not unreservedly admit that man began as a savage are supposed to hold that man was created a perfect and almost angelic being . . . or as a child."[10]

Müller argues that we simply don't have enough evidence to decide what human beings began as: "Disappointing as it may sound, the fact must be faced, nevertheless, that our reasoning faculties, wonderful as they are, break down completely before all problems concerning the origin of things." He anticipated the modern position that, since all religions postulate stories both mythological and historical about human beginnings and since it really is difficult to "prove" any of the stories scientifically, we must, both as scholars and human beings, respect them all.

This position has two implications. One is that scholars rarely use words like *primitive* and *archaic* for chronologically older religions. More acceptable terms include *indigenous* and *tribal*. Although some scholars do recognize developmental schemes in religions, they are careful to note that they do not mean by this that newer necessarily means better.

The second implication is that respect must pertain even if we disagree with someone personally. When you looked at the three alternatives Müller offered about how human beings began—perfect, childlike, savage—I'm sure you suddenly had strong feelings about which would comport the best with your personal religious beliefs. This brings us to our second word.

Humility

Science and religion have had their disagreements over the years, but on one point they should find perfect harmony. Both should instill in their practitioners and theorists a great deal of humility. The fact that they don't, that there is no shortage of either arrogant scientists or arrogant theologians, should not deflect us from the central point: humility is a key attitude.

Scientists should be humble simply in the face of the history of science. Today's theories are tomorrow's historical curiosities. If rules are made to be broken, scientific theories are made to be superseded by new discoveries and better explanatory systems. Despite all the wonderful discoveries and inventions the past two hundred years of science have provided us, the frontiers of the still-to-be-discovered are as broad and deep as ever. The prospects for every scientist should be both exciting and humbling.

Theologians should be similarly humbled by their subject matter. All religions postulate the existence of a higher power or interpretive principle. For almost all, that power or principle has indefinable elements. In Christian theology, for example, certain things about God's nature and purpose can be known—enough for us to know God's requirements, is how it is usually stated—but other things may not be known.

Human beings cannot fully fathom the extraordinary nature of God. This element of mystery, combined with our human status as creatures in the Creator-creature relationship, means that humility is the only proper response in the face of God's existence.

What this means is that on two, perhaps three, counts the scholar of religion should demonstrate humility—both as scientist and as student of religion. If those inside a religious tradition are humbled by the depth of its subject matter, how much more so should those outside the tradition be humbled.

But perhaps the third count is the most important, because all of us come to the task of religious studies with a faith commitment of our own. The discipline does not require that we give up that commitment. As we saw in the last chapter, the best students of religion are those who recognize their commitment and are able to use it as firm ground from which to respectfully study other systems of commitment. But the field of religious studies does require that we not let our own commitment in any way contribute to falsifying the data we collect about other religions. And humility is a helpful tool to prevent our own faith commitment from becoming a means of even unintentional untruthfulness.

This does not mean that we are in any way minimizing the importance of what we believe or our commitment to it. It simply means that humility is a way of doing a reality check. For Christians it means that even though we may think our religion is the one, true religion, we still don't know everything there is to know about God. In fact, we know only a tiny fraction of all there is to know about God. This recognition is humility. It helps us to respect other human beings with different beliefs and to be open and sensitive to their concerns.

Sensitivity

Sensitivity cuts two ways. I remember reading one of my first religious studies textbooks, and the authors suggested in that textbook that Abraham was probably an eponymous character. When I looked up eponymous, I discovered it meant "representative of a group of similar people." Abraham, these authors were saying, was not a single person, but many people, and this name represented a whole class of people who all migrated from the eastern lavant to the western, who were leaders of large extended families or tribes, and who eventually coalesced to found a new nation that came to be called Israel.[11]

I was shocked. Abraham was my hero. The moving story of his willingness to sacrifice his son Isaac was one of my favorites in all of Scripture. When I thought of faithfulness, I thought of Abraham. I even had in mind a picture of what this wonderful person looked like. And now this author was suggesting that this person didn't really exist in the way I thought he did.

When I began to teach world religions classes to college and then seminary students, I learned another lesson in sensitivity. I always started my classes with the great Eastern religions—Hinduism, Confucianism, and Buddhism—and then slowly worked my way west. I prided myself on being respectful, humble, clear, and truthful as I described these belief systems that were not my own and were not the religious traditions of my largely Christian students. The first half of the class usually went swimmingly: I told the stories of Buddha, Mahavira, and Confucius; I described their great achievements and some of the stories that grew up around these larger-than-life figures. The students felt comfortable with this engaging (I'm sure) recitation. But when we got to Judaism and Christianity, to the stories of Moses, Jesus, and Paul, the mood always changed. I don't think I varied my teaching technique one bit—the same format, the same historical recitation of what happened. But the students did not smile knowingly in the same way when I described Paul's interesting personality quirks. Moses' temper tantrum, as I engagingly termed it, when he came down from Sinai and discovered the golden calf, was serious stuff. And I was not being as serious as my students wanted me to be.

The beginning religious studies scholar is almost never sensitive enough about other people's religious beliefs and almost always too sensitive about his or her own. A good rule of thumb is for you to expect to have to make a great effort on two fronts. First, go out of your way to describe other people's religious beliefs in charitable, understanding terms. Second, realize that, if your religion is as true as you think it is, it will withstand a great deal of honest, objective scrutiny. However, for a long time, honest, objective scrutiny will seem suspiciously like blasphemy to you. Get used to it. And if you do, I can promise you two things. You will become a better scholar for it. And, more importantly, your personal faith will become stronger and even more meaningful to you.

A final thought: don't expect this to come easily. Remember that sensitivity is a two-way street. People in other religious traditions come at their studies in the same way you come at yours. Blasphemy, like sensitivity, also cuts two ways: what may seem to you like the fairest possible explanation of another religious tradition may seem totally biased to its followers. Trying to arrive at explanations that satisfy both parties takes hard work.

Advocacy

Does championing one religious tradition over another have any place in the scholarly study of religion? The answer to that, especially in the data collection stage, is no. To many of you this will seem like a simple and logical answer. But to others of you it will confirm your worst fears: namely, that by becoming a religious studies scholar, you are being expected to give up an essential element of your faith. Let me make three comments that I hope will be of help in this matter.[12]

First, all religions are in some sense missionary religions. All advocate. All teach that their way is the right way.

Some are more intentional about the missionary urge. Of the major world religions, Christianity, Buddhism, and Islam are often termed the missionary religions, because their founders told their followers explicitly to go and preach the gospel/dhamma/quran. But the other world religions, and in their own way the indigenous religions, are missionary also. They all describe reality in a way they think is true. Sometimes they believe that their tribe or group has a special place in that description of reality and that "God" has made other provisions for other peoples. But that belief in itself is a way of determining for others what their religious destiny should be in terms of the destiny of the enlightened ones. If you don't believe this, there is a simple way to test it: challenge followers of one of the so-called nonmissionary religions on the way they describe the world. You will discover an extremely strong attachment to their description and to all of our places in it.

Since all religions are missionary religions in some sense, no tradition needs to apologize for its missionary urge. There is a movement afoot that teaches that none of the religions should be missionary religions. But this movement has a religious fervor of its own about it; that is to say, it is a mission in itself. It is promoted by those who hold and teach it to be the best description of the way things should be—for everyone. As a missionary message, it needs to be taken seriously, understood, and evaluated, like any other form of witness and religious belief. But acceptance of it is not a requirement for doing religious studies.

Second, if all religions are missionary religions, then the question we face is not whether proselytizing should be done, but when.

Religious studies methodology suggests that missionary activity is not a part of religious studies. Thus, one doing religious studies holds in abeyance the missionary urge, either by doing it prior to study or doing it after study or allowing that someone else will be doing it or recognizing that it has already been done.

Third, equally important is the question of how missionary activity is done.

As important as the timing question is the question of how missions should be done. One way to answer this question would be to say that it is none of the business of the religious scholar. That may be correct. I wonder, however, if this is not something about which the study of religion should have a great deal to say, particularly on the historical study of missions in the different religions. Often, missions has been a positive world force. At other times it has not. Some helpful research and commentary from religious studies scholars might be forthcoming on the issue.

The questions of advocacy naturally lead one toward the questions of criteria of good and bad religions—in short, the questions of truth. These are valid questions for the religious studies scholar. But they are later rather than earlier questions. Scholars go through the steps of collecting information and explaining it accurately before they undertake the task of valuation. We will do the same and will address the question of truth in chapter 8.

EXERCISE

Write a one-page historical sketch of the life of Muhammad and a one-page historical sketch of the life of Jesus. Compare the two, and write a one-page analysis of differences between the two as you have written them.

Part **2**

Observing

4

Determining the Religious Event

efore starting a religious studies project, you must do some essential preliminary work. Reading chapter 1 will have helped you to define *religion* in a way that will allow you to be most efficient with your project. Now you must do something further: locate the object of your study in time and space and determine the structure and function of the belief or practice you will research.

Other disciplines might call this locating process "limiting the subject." Religious studies is a huge field, and if you hope to carry out a valid research project, you must cut down the field to a manageable size. An analogy might help.

The most difficult decision for someone wishing to drill an oil well is where to drill. Since an oil well is an expensive undertaking, drillers spend a great deal of time researching the possible locations by analyzing the topography of the area, the results of previous drilling in the area, and other signs and signals that might indicate where the oil lies. Only after all this preliminary work is done does the drilling commence.

The religious studies scholar does similar pre-project research. The field of religion is as wide open as the fields in which oilmen choose to drill. You can't drill everywhere, and choices made before the study begins will make a difference in the focus and value of the project. Religions and religious practices are as numerous as the possible locations of an oil well. Homing in on the one to study and then placing it in the context of the entire field is an important first step.[1] Traditionally, this locating process in religious studies considers all three factors mentioned at the beginning of this chapter: time, place, and structure.

Time: The Influence of Development

Religion is not static. It changes. Religion itself changes, religious people change, and the cultures that carry religions change. Therefore, if you want to study a religious practice or belief, the first thing to do is to locate it in this process of historical change.[2]

Sometimes this time location is important as background information. It is essential, for example, to know that the Buddha grew up in a privileged home of nobles and that many of his early teachings have an anti-institutional cast that reflect his rejection of that home life. Later in his teaching career he had to deal with a growing number of followers who needed to be organized, directed, and disciplined. The Buddha began to teach on these subjects, out of necessity, in a way that would probably have never occurred to him as a young man. The time of his teaching is an important factor to consider in understanding his teaching.[3]

Sometimes this time location is important in order to understand the development of a doctrine. Early in Muhammad's career as a street preacher in Mecca, he taught about a concept known as *jihad* in terms of individual, internal spiritual warfare. Later, when Muhammad had developed a large following and had gained some political as well as spiritual authority, his teachings on *jihad* took on a more outward, social cast. Both of these early and late teachings are present in the Quran. Knowing the timing of each adds a richness and depth to the teaching of *jihad* that Muslim theologians grapple with today.[4]

You should know as a religious studies scholar that different religious groups are more or less open to the concept of religious practices developing (or not developing) in time. Groups that emphasize revelation from God or the Eternal tend to downplay developmental themes, particularly as they relate to doctrine. These religious groups emphasize the once-for-all revelation and the unchangeableness of the doctrine as it is received from God. Most of these groups, however, do acknowledge that human understanding of the divine revelations changes, often growing in depth and application over time.[5]

Other groups view all religion as a product of developmental forces; in fact, some of these groups view nothing about religion as unchanging or solid. Everything is a function of time, and to speak of any enduring essence is a mistake.[6]

As a religious studies scholar you will probably find yourself striking a happy medium between these two positions. Most scholars recognize that there are some consistent elements within each religion that give it special identity[7] (making Christianity Christianity, for example, no matter what the time or place), but that all religions do change over time and it is essential to understand the broad sweep of those changes.

How do you carry out this time-locating task? Let's say that you have an idea that you want to study Christian conversion in the nineteenth century. The first step is to get a sense of the full sweep of conversion as it has been viewed throughout Christian history. Unless you are writing a thesis on the subject and are prepared to read eighty to a hundred books, a good place to start would be articles in religion encyclope-

dias.[8] Look under "conversion, Christian." Encyclopedia articles tend to be overviews and will give you a good sense of
what conversion has meant in Christian circles during the
major periods of Christian history. Time needed: one hour.
Key question: Where does this belief or practice fit in the
overall developmental pattern of this particular religious tradition?

②   A second step is to read more specific material on the period
of your study. This might be a chapter in a book on nineteenth-century Christianity. A good place to start here is the
bibliography that was probably attached to the encyclopedia
article. Another option is to write or call an expert or two in
the field (again, names might be at the end of the encyclopedia article) and ask them what they consider to be the best
concise summary of the period in question.[9] Time needed:
two hours, although the task may be spread out over a number of days because of the correspondence involved. Key question: What is distinctive about this belief or practice during
this time period?

③   Third, in the course of your reading you may find more
specific information that you need to follow up. Perhaps you
will discover that someone has written an article titled or sub-
titled "Christian Conversion in the Nineteenth Century," the
exact topic of your prospective work. Reading this article, of
course, is a must. It could lead you in one of several possible
directions. It may convince you that your topic is covered
already and you need to change. That will seldom happen,
however, because there will almost always be something about
the subject that you want to investigate but the author has
not dealt with. This primary work, however, may force you
to focus your project more sharply than you had intended.
Time needed: variable. Key question: How does the time-
location question affect my project as I have formulated it?

One final note on time location: different religions have
different views of the function of time. Western religions view

time as linear, moving from starting point A to the present B to a culminating point C sometime in the future. Eastern religions don't view religious time as moving in that same way. For religions like Hinduism and Buddhism, time tends to move in repeatable sequences, spirals, or circles, rather than straight lines. In one sense, this does not change the way we view time as we do our scholarly research. When placed in secular, historical time, these religions do have religious histories that can be understood as linear. In another important sense, however, it has a great deal to do with our research method. Adherents of these religions, because they view sacred time differently, behave differently, and that perception and practice must be factored into our understanding of time development.[10]

Place: The Influence of Culture

When we consider the factor of time, we are considering mostly the influence of development within the history of a particular religious tradition. The factor of place focuses more on the relationship between a religion and the culture in which it thrives (or survives).[11]

For example, it is essential that the student of Buddhism understand that when the Buddha started his teaching in sixth-century India he was addressing a culture that in some ways was becoming dissatisfied with the prevailing Hindu culture. The Brahmanical sacrificial cult had become so elaborate and expensive that many of the temple sacrifices were out of reach of the average Indian. When seen in this light, the Buddha's teachings on the importance of individual spiritual effort that relies on "coming and seeing" the truth for oneself and then doing something about it oneself, become much more understandable. Knowing the cultural context also makes it easier to understand why the Buddha's teaching met with initial success.[12]

Another example: the New Age movement appeals to a large number of Americans. On the one hand, this seems odd since, to many of us "enlightened" modern thinkers, some of Shirley MacLaine's pronouncements seem, shall we say, esoteric. On the other hand, when the teachings of the New Age are understood in the context of a spiritually starved, secular culture that has systematically attempted to remove the supernatural element from public life, the thirst for New Age esoterica and the hope of reaching out and touching all different kinds of spiritual beings and realities become understandable.[13] The prevailing culture often creates itches that new and different religious beliefs scratch.

Some religious studies scholars have felt that the cultural element to religion has been too long overlooked. They have emphasized it in recent works, particularly in dealing with the phenomenon of who belongs to what religion. John Hick, in *An Interpretation of Religion*, says that "in some ninety-nine percent of the cases the religion which an individual professes and to which he or she adheres depends upon the accidents of birth."[14] Hick and others have probably rightly corrected a real lack in the study of religion—that is, realistic assessment of the influences of culture on religion and religious membership. But in so doing, they may have overstated the case.

This perceived overstatement has led other scholars to think that the unique, revelatory aspect of religion has gotten shortchanged in the process. Did not God (or Brahman or Allah or Yahweh) really speak, and is it not the eternal, unchanging aspect of what was spoken that should be the focus of our research?[15]

Religious studies scholars do well to take both culture and revelation into account in their work. No religious tradition is able to express itself without using some cultural form to do so. In fact, many use scores of cultural forms. So both culture and revealed truth are necessary to adequately describe a religion.

The good news for the beginning scholar is that with all this emphasis on cultural influences, determining the context of a particular religion is not all that difficult today. The first step is to search for written material that describes the cultural influence on your chosen topic. Let's say that you want to study the effect of Japanese culture and religion on emperor worship in Shinto. Due largely to the importance of this subject in Western trade and the events of World War II, it is not difficult to find such analyses. About two hours' worth of reading should give you a beginning perspective on how Shinto has always been a unique feature of Japanese nationalism.[16] Key question: Why has this religious belief been an important one in this particular culture?

There may not be written analyses of the relationship between religion and culture for your particular project. In that case, you will have to provide it yourself by studying the culture of the time period in question and comparing your findings with the religious teaching. This may become an auxiliary project in itself. Even if it is only a small part of your research, it can become an important contribution.

A second step in our sample project on Shinto would be to isolate from your reading the role that emperor worship has played in Japanese religion and culture. Has it always been mandatory? Has the relative importance of nationalism and religious belief always been evenly balanced, or have the two varied in emphasis depending on the cultural, political, and economic situation? What are the key factors today? Key question: What role(s) has this practice played in this culture?

A third step might be to try to determine the variety of opinions today, from Japanese people first and from others second, on the status of this belief. Has it changed? Is it growing in importance in the system? Or has it been largely relocated in the tradition, or deemphasized? Key question: What is the status of this belief in this place today?

The relationship between religion and culture has been a tricky one. At different times, scholarly opinion has made one subservient to another and vice versa. Both religion and culture are notoriously difficult to define—religion for reasons outlined in chapter 1, culture because by its very nature it is so transitory and changeable, and its boundaries from one group of people to the next is so difficult to determine. It stands to reason that, given this difficulty with their definitions, the question of their relationship should be problematic. But in this day of truly world religions, of more and more religions having the opportunity to be cross-cultural entities, there is no question more on the cutting edge than that of the relationship between the two.

Structure: The Importance of Function

When locating a particular religious belief or practice in time and space, we limit ourselves mainly to that religion. We first consider the historical sweep of the religion, and then we consider the relationship between that religion and culture. Next we should consider the belief or practice chosen for study in comparison with similar practices in other religions. This is called looking at a religious practice phenomenologically.[17]

At this stage of pre-project research, what you should do is not a formal compare-and-contrast procedure, common to comparative religion methodology. We will discuss that in detail in chapter 7. Right now you just want to get an idea of the phenomenon you are about to consider and get a general impression of how widespread it is in the whole field of religion.

For example, the idea of salvation or liberation is common in most of the world's religions. But the idea has different features in different religions, so much so that it would be a mistake to consider Christian salvation and Hindu *moksha* (liberation) as synonymous. Christian salvation is an escape from sin, both willful and original, while Hindu *moksha* is not freedom from sin but liberation from ignorance, from a false way of looking at the world. Still, the ideas are obviously related. They are related most closely in the function they perform in Christianity and Hinduism. Each is the vehicle by which human life is transformed from an unacceptable state to an acceptable one. Since most religions have a similar vehicle, it is fair to ask of new religions: Do you have anything that performs the salvation/liberation function?

Another example is the concept of God or of a transcendent force or idea. Almost all religions seem to have one. It performs the function of representing ultimate reality. Sometimes this reality acts personally to intervene in the lives of human beings; at other times it acts more impersonally, as a model or a "retired" high god. In spite of the similarities, the differences between the ultimates are pronounced enough to prevent us from considering them synonymous. God, Yahweh, Allah, Brahman, Dhamma, Wakon Tonka, the Tao, and others have different personalities (or no personalities) and behave in different ways. Their similar functions in the structure of their religions are enough to classify them together, but their differences are pronounced.

For some scholars, this structural approach to studying the world religions is the best way, the way that allows religion to set itself apart from the other disciplines such as psychology, history, and sociology. It treats phenomena as *sui generis* religious, unique in their own right.

Other scholars find the comparative, phenomenological approach to be needlessly analytical. It slices up religions in ways they should not be parsed. Remove Hindu *moksha* from the total religious system, for example, and it can easily be misunderstood; it can be understood only when seen within the full spectrum of Hindu thought. Trying to isolate phenomena is like taking squares of fabric from little girls' dresses, as my wife's grandmother did, and stitching them together to make a quilt. She produced a nice quilt. But it has nothing to do with little girls' dresses. We cannot really get an understanding of dresses from the quilt.

Those who limit religious studies to phenomenology and those who reject phenomenology are both taking extreme positions. Surely, this systematic approach to all the world's religious practices has value, as long as it is remembered that the practices and the beliefs themselves cannot be fully understood unless known in their natural settings, in their total religious settings.[18]

So why do we survey similar religious practices as we begin our religious studies research projects? We do it because we can learn a lot about a single isolated practice from seeing it alongside other similar practices. Even if our study is not, strictly speaking, a comparative one, we can still gain a great deal of depth of understanding through systematic comparison.

Let's say we want to do a study of transcendental meditation.[19] Our first step is to try to understand in a preliminary way the role T.M. plays in the lives of its practitioners. Is it strictly therapeutic? Does it connect them with the transcendent? What benefits accrue to the practitioner? It should not be difficult to find a magazine article or book chapter written by a recognized authority, outlining the role T.M. plays. Key question: What is the primary function of T.M. in the religious lives of its practitioners?

The second step, once we have satisfied ourselves as to T.M.'s role, is to find the general category that subsumes this function and appears in some or most other religions. In the case of T.M. the category might be prayer, for example, or it might be a category that includes confession and catharsis. Whatever you determine it is that serves the primary function, you should then read a survey article or two that will give you a general idea of the variety of practices included in this function.

Perhaps this chapter sounds more complicated than it really is—because all the ideas here are probably new to you as a beginning student, I have done more explaining of them than will seem necessary after you have done a few religious studies research projects. Soon you will instinctively be able to answer the key questions of the chapter and will be able to locate your subject matter quite accurately with a quick read of a few well-chosen articles.

Remember, the work described in this chapter is largely preliminary. The research you do at this stage may never be presented in your finished project. Or it may appear only in summary form as you describe your project at the beginning of your paper. But doing this work is important. It can prevent a great deal of misstepping later on as you get into your project. And it will make getting over the rough spots of research much easier. It will give you a good idea of the lay of the land surrounding your topic and thus will enable you to find the resources you need to solve problems quickly.

EXERCISE

Select one of the following topics and locate it in time, place, and function in the religious world:

Prayer: *The Devotio Moderna* in Fifteenth-Century Roman Catholic Piety

Scriptures: The Importance of the Arabic Language to Muslim Understandings of the Quran

Heaven: The Confucian Mandate of Heaven

Hermits: The Forest Dwelling Stage of the Hindu Life Cycle

Pilgrimage: The Function of Holy Relics in Early Buddhism

5

Talking to People about Religion

eligion is about people. This means that when we study religion we are studying people. But it means more than that. It also means that some of the best sources of information for the study of religion are people themselves. But there is some skill involved in learning about religion from people.

The Varieties of Human Resources on Religion

At the beginning stages of a religious studies project there is no greater help than talking to an *expert* in the religious tradition or religious phenomenon you are about to study. Such a person can give you invaluable advice about the difficulty (or ease) of your project, the problems you can expect to find, the work that has been done in that area already, and resources you can use. These resources might include bibliographies, other experts, and information from churches, mosques, and temples. Whether your adviser is an expert by confession or by academic specialty, he or she will likely have trod at least part of the ground you are preparing to walk.

On the other hand, there are times and subjects where the people you will want to talk to are not experts in the field, but are *practitioners* of the tradition. Sometimes the data you want to collect is behavioral or affective in nature: You may want to know what it feels like to be converted to Christianity, what a worshiper of Vishnu knows about his or her god, what true submission to Allah means in the everyday life of a businessman. The expert is of little help here; the practitioner can tell you what you want to know, and then it is up to you to process the data.

There are several ways to collect this kind of data. One is the person-to-person interview. Interviews are best if the data required are somewhat complicated and subjective. How you feel about God, in your own words, can be powerful in the telling. An interview also has the most flexible format for gathering data, in that you can depart from prepared questions if it becomes evident that they have little meaning for the interviewee or that he or she has a better story to tell about something else. If the data you hope to collect in interviews will have to be quantified somehow, it is best to start with a list of prepared questions and work your way through them—but feel free to depart from the format and follow interesting trails of information. One limitation of the interview is its expense, both in money and time. This generally cuts down on the number of contacts and the amount of information you can collect.[1]

A second data collection technique to use with practitioners is observation. Perhaps you are interested in the practice of prayer in a certain religion, particularly the postures and public formats used in prayer. Watching a certain number of adherents pray, recording your observations, and drawing conclusions from what you observe is a valid research technique. It avoids one subjective factor common to a verbal interview, the tendency of people to tell you either the ideal they would like to practice or what they think you would like to hear about their practice. In observation you are in control of the situation, and the only bias you must allow for is yours as an observer. The weakness of observation, of course, is that you are limited to external behavior. For understanding some religious practices, that is enough. For many others, the external must be matched with the internal motivation and comprehension that can only be inferred from your observations.[2]

A third data collection technique is the written questionnaire. The first religious studies questionnaires were developed by an American, E. D. Starbuck, a Harvard psychologist of religion in the early twentieth century. Questionnaires overcome many of the limitations of interviews and observation: A well-written questionnaire can reduce the amount of subjective bias on the part of both the interviewee and interviewer; it reduces cost and allows you to get to thousands more practitioners, if that is the kind of information desired; it is also easily quantifiable, and today with computer processing it allows for fast and accurate cross-tabulations on many different variables.[3]

All three techniques—interviews, observations, questionnaires—can reveal important insights on religious behavior. Consider, for example, the research done by Gordon Allport on the subject of church attendance and prejudice. Prior to Allport, findings by psychologists of religion had reported a positive correlation between church attendance and prejudice against minorities. People who attended church regularly tended to display more prejudice. Allport questioned these findings. Using both interviews and questionnaires, Allport discovered that the two were not related in a direct cause-and-effect way—that is, going to church and accepting Christian theology were not direct causes of increased prejudice. Allport found that another psychological need, common to a high percentage of churchgoers and prejudiced people, made it appear that the two were related. But religious practice itself did not lead to prejudice. This type of research into religious motivations lends itself to the questionnaire technique.[4]

A third group of people who can provide valuable data in religious studies includes the *religiously neutral*, the *disinterested*, and the *hostile*. These non-religious subjects can give you "outsider" impressions of a religious tradition or practice. Of course the information you collect will have a distinct bias to it (or in some cases ignorance). But this doesn't invalidate the information. As long as the bias is well-defined, that is, as long as the group interviewed, observed, or surveyed is well-defined, then the information it supplies can be used in numerous ways.[5]

The Dangers of First-Person Information

Each of these groups and collection techniques has weaknesses as a source of information. It is important that you seek expert advice in how to collect and evaluate the data from any one of them. But several dangers lurk in dealing with all of them.

The first danger is to *overestimate the knowledge* of the people from whom you collect data. This is a particular danger when surveying practitioners. We automatically think that because someone is, say, a Muslim, that person knows a lot about the religion of Islam. In fact, most people have one-sided, incomplete understandings of their own religion. If you are a Christian, for example, think of the kind of answer you would get if you went to your church and tapped someone at random on the shoulder and asked him or her to give a short summary of Christianity. Many, if not most, Christians in the pews would give sketchy answers. Ditto for those of other religious traditions. So consider what kind of information you are getting when you consult the average religious person; it is real, but it is rarely authoritative or expert.

The second danger, particularly in the interview process, is *idiosyncratic information.* In interviewing, it is always nice to run across someone with articulate, interesting answers to your questions. Unfortunately, there is no guarantee that such a person is really representative of the group you are most interested in. In fact, such people are often those who are rebelling in some way from their traditional faith and have, as a result, read more and thought more about alternative versions of their faith than those who are quite satisfied with their religion. There are safeguards against idiosyncratic religious views, of course. One is the simple application of numbers—interviewing or polling enough people that the odd answers (what William James called "wild facts") don't get factored into the final conclusions.

A third danger is *advocacy*—the intentional or unintentional skewing of data because people want their religion to be seen in a good light. The people you are interviewing, observing, or polling are not usually scholars, trained to be objective and precise about data. They are probably people used to championing their faith. Thus, they might exaggerate and embellish—sometimes even prevaricate. A good data collector allows for this, of course. A well-written questionnaire can neutralize most advocacy by the structure, sequence, and number of its questions. But advocacy must be carefully factored into any results.

A fourth danger—headache, really—is *uncooperativeness*. Not everyone wants to be part of your research project. Not everyone likes to talk about his or her religion. Three reasons can account for the uncooperative response. The first is a desire for privacy. Many people do not consider religion a public thing to be discussed with strangers. They view their religion to be between themselves and the Eternal. If, after hearing you fully describe your project and its aims, people say they don't feel comfortable talking about their faith, so be it. A second reason for uncooperativeness is insecurity. Some people are not sure about their faith, and objective talk about it can be threatening. Insecurity can sometimes be overcome if you are reassuring in your manner. Explain the limited ways in which the data will be used. Offer anonymity if that is possible within the parameters of your research plan. (Sometimes it is, and sometimes it is not. Be honest.) Be supportive of the people you are dealing with, and assure them you are not in the least questioning their faith. They may come around. The third reason for uncooperativeness is hostility. Some people will simply not like you. Perhaps the reason will be because they do not trust someone who is not of their religion. Perhaps they see questions as threats. There may be many reasons. And there is little likelihood that you will change their minds.

Advantages of Person-to-Person Research

There are many advantages of person-to-person research, regardless of the nature of your project. My doctoral dissertation was a comparison of the monastic rule Buddhist *bhikkhus* in Sri Lanka live by and the Christian monastic rule written by Saint Basil in the fifth century.[6] The comparison was largely a literary and theological study; it could have been done from the cushy confines of my office in Evanston, Illinois. I was fortunate, however, to live for a year in Sri Lanka, and during the course of the year I interviewed hundreds of Buddhist experts, practicing monks, and even some people hostile to the Buddhist *sangha*, or order of monks (although there are not many in that country). As a result of these person-to-person contacts, I was able to understand parts of the Buddhist monastic rule that would have remained quite odd and foreign to me otherwise. My depth of understanding and insight increased tremendously, and I think the project was much improved.

Some projects, of course, cannot be done without person-to-person contact. We are not just talking about adding a nice touch and an increased depth of understanding; we are talking about projects that, because of their design and purpose, must use social science research methodologies and need a person-to-person technique to collect the necessary data.

There are other advantages to person-to-person research. Your study will gain increased credibility. Being able to report on a conversation with an expert in the field of your work means you took the time to get guidance. It means that someone well-versed in the field had a chance to comment on the project design, give his or her opinion on it, and perhaps even comment on the results. The credibility derived from such contact is enormous.

Your study will also demonstrate a great sympathy with adherents of the religions you are studying if you show you talked with practitioners of those religions. Nothing angers Christians more, for example, than commentary from people who have never had firsthand contact with Christians and are speaking from secondhand information and stereotypes. The same goes for people from other religions who don't feel they have been given a chance to have their say. Thus, a person-to-person data collection technique not only gets you more reliable data, it also gains you a great deal of sympathy and trust from those concerned.

Almost any religious studies project has a human element impossible to measure in any other way than firsthand contact. If there is an essence to religion, it lies somewhere in that ultimately indefinable area of human response to divine initiative or presence. Even if the aim of your project is to measure as mundane a subject as the financial support of a group of religious people, the human religious element needs to be factored in. There is a difference between charitable giving to support a religious group and support of the United Way. And although there will ultimately be an indefinable element to this difference in motivation, a researcher can learn more about it from person-to-person contact than from research limited to written and secondhand sources.[7]

In addition, future studies will be enhanced. It is in doing the research for one project that discoveries are made that indicate next steps. The likelihood of this happening is greatly increased the more first-person contact you have. Interpersonal contacts are unpredictable in many ways, and nuggets of information, nuances of thought, and unexplored problem areas will always lie waiting for those who take the trouble to make such contacts.

Basic Rules for Person-to-Person Research

Be clear about what you are after. There is a place for random, exploratory information gathering in interpersonal research, but if that is your intent, be frank about it, both with yourself and with the people you are talking to. Usually you should have done enough preliminary research and reading to know exactly the information you want. You should be able to describe your goals clearly and succinctly to the people you talk to, observe, or poll. People are much more forthcoming with information if you tell them what it is you seek. If they trust you and believe in your project, they will usually go out of their way to help. They will feel part of the research team.

Be realistic about what you can expect. It is only after you know what information you are looking for that you choose the people to seek it from. There is nothing more frustrating in person-to-person research than trying to get information from people who do not have it or, if they do, are incapable of articulating it. The feelings of failure in such cases extend beyond yourself. They infect the people whom you are interviewing. Don't overestimate what a group of people can deliver. Set realistic goals. And make sure you use the interviewing technique or questionnaire that can deliver the information you need.

Don't rush to judgment. The time period immediately after collecting your data is good for some things and not good for others. After an interview, for example, is an excellent time to go over your notes or tape and make corrections, additions, or notations about observations that occurred to you during the interview but you did not have time to record. The information is still fresh, your adrenaline is still high, and you can capture insights that you will not be able to recall later. However, this is not the time to make sweeping judgments about what you have just experienced and the data you have just collected. Good and bad feelings about the data and the person interviewed need to be captured for later evaluation, but those same feelings are too strong right after the interview to allow for much more; they will skew and color the data if you attempt an immediate evaluation. Write your feelings down, and then let the material sit for a period of time.

Don't naively accept everything your sources tell you. This may seem to be the converse of the previous rule about not rushing to judgment. In a sense, a good religious studies scholar looks for the best as he or she collects data: "If you want to know how a religious system other than your own deals with things, do not start with a book written to refute that system. Read one written by someone who believes it. Allow that other person the benefit of the doubt. Let the other person represent the religion in the best possible light," is the way a team of experienced researchers, John F. Wilson and W. Royce Clark, put it. But they also caution about going overboard in acceptance: "There is another kind of nonlistener—the gullible one. This person does not really want an explanation. He or she is looking for a guru, to believe what the guru says to believe. This is a kind of emotional and intellectual escape method that says, 'I'll accept that because I like you.' . . . That means that no communication is taking place, and it probably also means that you are developing some distorted ideas about what the other person believes."[8] If during an interview the subject says something you don't understand or don't trust, ask a clarifying question. Do not jump to judgment, but make sure you understand the answer and make sure that you give the interviewee a chance to explain himself or herself without needlessly feeling challenged.

Keep careful records. Make sure you have a system that identifies where information came from and records as exactly as possible what was said. Your procedure must be complete enough that if you come back to this information a year from now—or five years from now—it will be clear and usable. The key questions: Who said this? Where? When? To whom? What exactly was said?

A Note on Personal Influences

Even the least subjective of the sciences, like physics and mathematics, are coming to recognize more and more the unavoidable role that the emotions, insight, intuition, and cultural background of the scientist play in research.[9] Some kind of influence from these factors is a given. Increasingly, this influence is seen as productive, if it is fully articulated and allowed for in experimental design.

The role of personal influence in religious studies is even more pronounced. This is partly because religious studies, as we have seen, uses more of the techniques of the social sciences than of the hard sciences. In the social sciences, the role of the subjective is pronounced. Objectivity is still sought. But the interaction between the objective and the subjective is much more a part of the process than it is in the hard sciences.[10]

In religious studies this factor is complicated further. As we have discussed on several occasions, there is an indefinable element to religion. The Eternal, the ultimate reality of religion, cannot be defined fully. Thus, even if the human response to that eternal reality can be fully mapped and charted (itself a questionable proposition), we are still left short in fully describing the religious event. In psychological terms, if an "event" has two halves, the stimulus and the response, then in religious studies only the response can be measured adequately. The stimulus can be described by the respondent and that description can be compared with other respondents' descriptions. From that comparison, some kind of norm can be articulated. But still, an element of mystery about the stimulus half of the equation remains.

This means that, in religious studies, the researcher's religious feelings about the Eternal, the stimulus, have the potential to play a larger than normal role (if normal is the typical scientific posture). I think this has both good and bad prospects.

First, the bad. The religious studies scholar must be a scholar in every sense of that term. There can be no question of the striving to collect bias-free data, of being open and honest in that collection, or of being a trustworthy deliverer of information that can be used, sought again, and then evaluated. If at any point of this conceptualizing, collecting, and collating process the researcher allows his or her perceptions or techniques to become skewed because of personal religious bias, then that person has failed as a scholar (and, I would suggest, as a religious person, since most religions hold up honesty as a positive value).

Now, the good. Because at some point, usually in the last or evaluation stage, the religious studies scholar must factor in the influence of the ineffable core of religion, the religious person who has firsthand experience of that ineffable core is in a better position to do this sensitively. Obviously, there are still dangers here. Even the most sensitive religious person runs the danger of imposing his or her conception of the Eternal on the person being consulted, whose conception and experience might be quite different. That would be incorrect and would lead to false results. But the religiously sensitive researcher, having made the attempt in his or her own life to relate to the sacred and the mundane elements, can be more alert to the problems and potentials of another person's attempts to do that than a person who has no religious experience. This might mean asking better questions, probing for otherwise hidden information, or even just exuding a sense of trustworthiness that might act as a catalyst in the research process.[11]

EXERCISE

Interview a classmate or a friend about a religious topic. Plan on a twenty-minute interview, and then write up the results in a five-page paper. Include in the paper a statement of the interview time, location, and subject, and a description both physical and biographical of the interviewee. End with a transcript or summary of the interview itself, in question-and-answer format.

The subject of the interview could be one of many things. Consider the following set of questions, based on issues raised in James McClendon's book Biography as Theology *(Philadelphia: Trinity, 1990), as one possibility. But feel free to vary this according to your interests—or to do something altogether different.*

What are your main spiritual and theological images? (For example, if the subject is a Christian, you might ask him or her to consider Jesus: Is your mental image of Jesus on the cross? In the garden of Gethsemane? Preaching?)

How do these key images apply to your life?

How do your images apply to your religious community's life?

What parts of your religious tradition are most important to your spiritual life? Give an example.

What parts of your tradition are not so important to your spiritual life? Example?

6

Dissecting the Religious Elements of a Culture

After reading the history of Hinduism and Buddhism, one cannot help but be struck by a radical difference in their development: Hinduism for most of its history has been a largely Indian religion. Until very recently, it has not spread beyond the cultural and political boundaries of India. Even today, although Hinduism is gradually becoming something of a worldwide phenomenon, the vast majority of Hindus still live in India.[1] Buddhism, on the other hand, has spread far beyond the borders of its native India. It spread early to Sri Lanka and then to Southeast Asia (notably, modern Burma, Thailand, Cambodia, Vietnam, and Laos). Early in the second century A.D. it went to China, then Japan and Tibet. In our day it has become firmly entrenched in Western Europe and the United States.[2]

This sharp difference—between Hinduism's early parochialism and Buddhism's apparent universality—raises questions about an important feature of all the world's religions: their close relationship to culture. As a part of a culture, religion takes on a shape that conforms to that culture. Sometimes the religion takes on so many features of the culture or the religion affects the culture so thoroughly that the two become almost indistinguishable. Historically, Hinduism and Indian culture have formed such a bond, and that is one reason Hinduism has not spread far beyond the borders of India.[3]

Some religions don't form such a tight relationship. Somehow these religions are able to move from culture to culture, taking with them a core set of beliefs and practices that remain identifiable, yet at the same time showing an ability to take on cultural elements that will make those beliefs and practices congenial to the resident populace. Religions that do this most easily are often called culturally adaptable religions.[4]

One reason Buddhism has been able to move from culture to culture is that it has always adapted itself to the local culture without compromising its essence. Christianity is another worldwide religion that has shown itself to be culturally adaptable. Both Buddhism and Christianity are worldwide religions with easily identifiable sets of core beliefs and practices, but both have also taken on an extraordinary number of forms by adapting to cultural features in different geographic locations.

The spread—or nonspread—of religions is an interesting topic with conflicting explanatory theories. I call my own theory of why some religions spread and others don't the McDonald's Theory.[5] Religions that lend themselves readily to categorizing and definition, particularly in the area of doctrine, spread more easily because the core is easily defined and the cultural accoutrements can be added and adapted. One of the reasons McDonald's has been so successful is that one can go into any McDonald's restaurant in the world and know the hamburger will taste the same. Religions that are able to maintain such quality control, independent of local tastes (although the architecture of a McDonald's is adapted to fit the culture) can spread easily. Other religions are more like unique restaurants that work only in a particular culture because their essence is tied so tightly to that culture. Take away the culturally determined essence, and the religion wilts. Zoroastrianism in Persia (now Iran) and Shinto in Japan come to mind as examples of this kind of religion. To complete the analogy, I suppose we should recognize "family picnic" religions that are portable but appeal only to certain groups of people who by choice remain fairly separate from the mainstream culture. Judaism might be the best example.

Because of this interesting relationship between culture and religion, and the strong implications it has for understanding the history of a faith or tradition, the student of religion must be adept at reading a culture religiously. That is, a student must learn to gather the information necessary to see what individual, corporate, and secondary manifestations of religion there are in a cultural setting. How do the individual residents of this area express their religious feelings in personal piety and everyday lives? What kinds of institutions—churches, mosques, temples, councils, and "parachurch," "paramosque," "paratemple," and "paracouncil" organizations—have grown up in this culture? In what ways have the religious impulses of the people of this area secondarily influenced the political, economic, and cultural structures of this society?

Only by learning about the individual, institutional, and secondary influences of a religion in an area can the religion scholar begin to get a sense of how the "theory" or "ideal" of a religion works its way out in the practice of the people and the structure of a society. Understanding religion in its human cultural context is seen more and more by scholars to be an indispensable element to understanding the keys to why some religions have survived and prospered and others have died.

To give you an idea of how this gathering of information on religion and culture works, let's do a study of a small town in Wisconsin. Mercer (pop. 1250) is located in northern Wisconsin and is in many ways a resort town oriented toward fishing in the spring and summer, hunting in the fall, and snowmobiling and cross-country skiing in the winter. I chose it as an example for three reasons:

1. It is small, and thus an idea of its religious structure can be communicated in the brief span of a chapter.
2. I had access to it in the summers of 1991 and 1992 when I was doing much of the writing on this book.
3. Many readers of this book will be able to identify with some aspects of the study easily because the town is so typically American midwestern in many of its features. Thus our profile will be very Christian and very American. But that should not lead you to think that the same kind of study could not be done anywhere in the world, after carefully substituting different names for the categories of research areas and carefully adjusting research techniques where the culture demands it.

Individual Manifestations

Before I begin my observations of Mercer, however, one further note on what we are doing. As was discussed in the last chapter, to discover what people do religiously, you must ask them or watch them. A religion scholar must know how to do both. People often will tell you one thing and do another—sometimes intentionally, sometimes without knowing it. Many times it is difficult for people to put into words what they do religiously. Therefore, watching them is necessary in order to fully describe their personal spiritual life.

This observation can be done at any of several different levels. Religious anthropologists often live for years at a time with the people they are studying, observing them practice their religions in both formal and informal settings and recording these observations until they have enough data to form general conclusions about overall patterns and the meanings of what they see people doing. On a shorter-term basis in Mercer, a religious scholar might observe people at worship and in small-group Bible studies in homes or might see what happens at a church softball game (although the latter will probably give a pretty low view of religion).

Watching what people do can be correlated with what they say about their faith. Listening to what people have to say can be done through surveys, if information from large numbers of people is desired, or through interviews, if a narrower, more in-depth understanding is the goal.

Don't overlook surveys that may have already been done of people in your study community. Sometimes churches will do surveys designed to find out what local people need and want in the way of church service. Often those surveys contain information about personal religious habits that can be useful. Of course, one must be careful to note the survey technique used—sample selection, question phrasing and sequence, method of approach—so that the information can be as bias-free as possible. Sometimes the area chamber of commerce or political governing board may have done surveys that can be used. At the very least, such surveys can help give direction to areas of inquiry.

From that information you can then design your own survey, homing in on more specific questions of your research interest. Such a survey can be done by phone (if most homes have phones) or door-to-door, if that is allowed. Check at city hall for regulations on door-to-door canvassing. If you have the budget for it, such surveys can also be done by mail. City hall might know what mailing lists are available. Perhaps you might also solicit volunteers through the local newspaper or bulletin board.

The general question being asked in our sample study is What are the people of Mercer like spiritually? What is the spiritual profile of the typical resident of Mercer?

Surveys, both existing ones and those you might design yourself, can give broad-based answers to our question. But more specific information may need to come through personal interviews, where you begin with a general set of questions but have the liberty to pursue in more detail the answers you get.

Don't overlook what you might learn from informal conversations. Begin a diary system in which you can record incidents and insights gained from everyday contacts with people in restaurants, stores, and on the street. Sometimes clues to religious behavior can come from the most unexpected conversations, and you must be alert to saving such serendipitous information.

Institutional Manifestations

Churches, temples, synagogues, and mosques are the obvious institutional manifestations of religions in any locale. In 1991 and 1992 Mercer had five churches from the following denominations: Wisconsin Evangelical Lutheran, Evangelical Lutheran Church of America, United Methodist, Church of the Nazarene, and Roman Catholic.

Generally, attending services of all religious institutions in the study community is extremely helpful to a scholar. After I attended the five Mercer churches, I jotted down the following informal notes. They will give you an idea of the kinds of things one might look for. Identifying themes from these first-time visits might guide subsequent visits and conversations with pastors and lay leaders.

Zion Evangelical Lutheran (Wisconsin Evangelical Lutheran). Small church packed full (60 people); good mix of ages; pastor middle-aged, active-looking; reminded of Lutheran practice of much of the liturgy done with back to people, facing altar; pastor preaches with full, rich voice, good gestures, great eye contact; content conservative, Scripture-based; no one greets me after service.

Faith Lutheran (Evangelical Lutheran Church of America). Large church, sanctuary wide and tall with open-beamed ceiling; pastor large man; 150 seats occupied by 62 people; sermon on the compassion of Jesus and what it means for us; several people greet me after service; church has a Saturday evening (5:30) service, probably catering to sports-minded locals and tourists alike.

Mercer United Methodist. Largely older people, about 60 attending in sanctuary that seats 300; request for help with annual turkey dinner; low-key service; woman pastor, middle-aged; strong children's sermon, good prayers; pastor inspires confidence with no-nonsense approach to liturgy and sermon; not greeted after service.

First Church of the Nazarene. Sallman's head of Christ behind pulpit; announcement of week-long revival services; 25 people, room for 130; young couples with young children; dominating organ music; pastor earnest, sermon on the need to live saintly lives, prayer produces saints; side issue of men being priests of their homes (obviously aimed at young families).

St. Isaac Jogues Roman Catholic. Two hundred people all ages; sense of excitement; as people enter most genuflect; older priest, careful measured phrases, clear, simple homily; offering taken on baskets on long sticks; young people assist with service and are active in liturgy. No one greets me afterward.

Follow-up discussions with the pastors are a must. Pastors and key lay leaders probably think as much as anyone about the spiritual make-up of a community and will have invaluable insights for you.

Attendance at more than one church service is necessary. I attended the Methodist church's turkey supper and rummage sale. Faith Lutheran Church had an early morning worship service by the lake. The Nazarene church had a week of revival services that were extremely revealing.

Some statistical comparisons also give clues to how the churches relate to the rest of the community. I often like to observe what I call the church/bar ratio in an area. (Mercer's is 5/6.) The easiest way to get this in a larger community is through a simple count in the yellow pages of "Churches" and "Bars." By the way, you also get a feel for the denominational (and religious) diversity of a community through checking the yellow pages. Let your fingers do the walking.

In addition, on your church visits you might determine the seats-available/seats-filled ratio (Mercer's is roughly 43 percent) and the Sunday morning people-in-church/people-at-home ratio (Mercer's is roughly 16 percent). None of these is definitive of a community's spirituality, of course, but taken together with all the other information you collect, they can be very interesting.

Parachurch institutions need exploring also. Food pantries, hospital charities, resale shops, prison ministries, and a whole host of other organizations often grow up from church bases, sometimes maintaining those ties, sometimes becoming independent nonprofit entities.

But perhaps as important and interesting as anything in a culture are the interactions between different religions. In some cultures this means contact between major world religions like Hinduism, Buddhism, and Islam. Although this kind of interaction has been foreign to largely Christian America in the past, it is becoming increasingly common here also, particularly in the larger cities where immigrant populations have brought their cultures and religions with them.[6]

Such was not the case in small-town, midwestern Mercer. But there was interaction of another kind. To describe that interaction, I must introduce another division of religions, a threefold division between indigenous, world, and modern religions.[7] Indigenous religions are the religions of the tribes and nations that occupied most lands before the time of modern nationalism. They emphasize the actions of the gods as they relate to the tribe, here and now, regarding prosperity and health. Native American and African Traditional religions are two good examples of subgroups of indigenous religions. World religions are those religions, most of which arose in the fifth century B.C.E., that emphasize the individual's standing before gods (or the transcendent) who promise a better time and place to come in the future. Hinduism, Buddhism, Judaism, Islam, and Christianity are the five largest world religions. Modern religions are those religions that arose in response to the upheaval, both intellectual and social, of modern times (usually seen as the period from the eighteenth-century European Enlightenment to the present). Bahai, Theosophy, Christian Science, and New Age religious movements in the United States are examples of modern religions.

Usually, when world religions clash with indigenous religions, the world religions supplant the indigenous. But the indigenous religions are never entirely removed. They influence the world religions, sometimes in unexpected ways. In our own culture today we see a revival of interest in Native American religions, and a few of their practices are being used in some Christian settings.[8]

Modern religions are attempts to fill lacunae left by world religions that have not adapted themselves to modern times. New Age, for example, is an interesting combination of Eastern religious metaphysics and Western individualism. Some modern religions last for a very short time; others become part of the ongoing culture.[9]

Whenever analyzing a culture, look for all three types of religions. In Mercer, I found Native American influences;

tribes in the area were having an impact on the culture in a number of ways: They fished in the lakes using nets in the off-season, which significantly reduced the fish population for sport fishermen. They opened gambling casinos. They became the subject of church meetings about promoting mutual understanding and evangelism. Local art in tourist shops reflected Native American themes. In all these ways and more, Native American relgion lived on as both an overt and a behind-the-scenes, unconscious influence.

I also found evidences of modern religion in the Mercer area. The nearby Munedowk Light Center provided guided retreats dealing with subjects like "Healing Your Inner Child," "A Course in Miracles," "T'ai-Chi," "Vegetarian Cooking," and "Astrology." This kind of eclectic collection is typical of what has come to be called New Age and is a Western attempt to incorporate Eastern religious teachings in a gnostic package. This influence on American religious culture is more pronounced than many think. Last year more than ten million Americans bought New Age products, such as rocks, crystals, pyramids, and charms. That doesn't mean that ten million Americans are New Agers, but the influence is pervasive.

In addition, there was a meditation center in Ironwood, a short drive from Mercer. Many Hindu-derived meditative practices have proved popular with stressed-out American consumers.

For the religious studies student the point is this: in analyzing a modern culture, you are likely to find at least some signs of indigenous, world, and modern religions. Your job is to assess the areas of and extent of influence that each one has.

Secondary Manifestations

Even the public, nonchurch sectors of a community can tell you a great deal about its spiritual make-up. Three elements are often identified: political, economic, and cultural.

Political. Governments have two responsibilities: keeping order and promoting the common good. How a particular government carries out those two tasks, and who it gets to do them, can give clues to the spiritual nature of a community.

Mercer has one of the finest fire departments anywhere, with modern trucks and equipment. With 1250 people, however, it considers having its own police protection too costly and relies on county protection. Finding out the process of how that decision was made by the city board might give clues to priorities, which in turn might give clues to recognizing the values most treasured by the people.

Other political questions might include: Is crime low and incidence of fire high? What is the nature of the crime that does occur? What benefits do citizens get from the city government? Are there city taxes? Are there any recent or ongoing scandals or frauds?

Economic. Mercer's economy is built on the tourist trade. This means that attractive local businesses that cater to the tourists are a must. Bars and supper clubs are common. Hardware stores, fishing tackle and bait shops, and sporting goods stores line the two main streets.

The local chamber of commerce, like most such organizations, meets to figure out ways to promote business. Like most small towns today, Mercer is in constant need of money, and so the chamber and the town board must consider all revenue-generating resources. That means that raffles and gambling, as allowed by Wisconsin state law, are considered. Some of these things can create moral dilemmas. What role do local religions play in helping resolve the moral elements of these issues? Are any of the pastors in town, for example, on the chamber of commerce or the city board?

Banks are often the financial backbone of a community. They provide a way for people to pool their money to be used for loans for community projects, small businesses, and personal development such as home ownership. The amount of money loaned and to whom is often a key to spiritual values.

Workforce statistics can also be telling. What is the unemployment rate? Who is unemployed? Is the unemployment rate higher for one particular ethnic group than for others? How about the unemployment rate for the young? The old?[10]

A Town Meeting[11]

I attended a town meeting to get a feel for how public business is done in Mercer. Sixty people crammed the small meeting hall. At the front sat eight commissioners—five men, three women. I later learned there was an unusually large turnout that day because a controversial discussion was to take place regarding all-terrain vehicles. That discussion led the agenda. The argument boiled down to danger versus money. "We don't want 'em," said one man. "I know the resort owners make money with the woods trails and all, but is it worth a couple of kids getting killed?" A committee was formed to discuss the issue further.

Several zoning variances were discussed. Most were to allow for exceptions to the rules governing the placement of wells and septic systems. All were granted: "They got to have water," was the typical rationale. The town chairman who ran the meeting, John Raabey, often encouraged input by saying something like, "This is your town, your meeting. What do you think?" The town has a small library, and the librarian asked for permission to use the town hall for children's storytelling hour Saturday mornings. Permission granted. Other issues discussed were waste disposal, a proposal to regrade a road on the edge of town, the change of a name of a road, and the ongoing need for a holding tank for water. After one and a half hours of discussion, the meeting adjourned.

Several of the issues raised had direct moral implications. The religious studies scholar could profitably follow up on several, noting how they were eventually resolved and whether discernible religious values had any role to play in the decision.

The overall goal of this sort of analysis is to paint a picture of the role religion plays in the lives of individuals and groups in any cultural setting. A good picture requires hard work, creativity, and time. But it can be an extremely interesting exercise.

EXERCISE

Train yourself to read the newspaper with an eye for religion. There is much to be learned about world affairs and the effects religion has on those affairs.

For one seven-day period, read a major newspaper (the New York Times, *the* Washington Post, *the* Wall Street Journal, *the* Christian Science Monitor) *and your local paper, looking for the influence of religion on the news. Identify stories with religious content, and then answer these questions:*

1. What role do religious ideas play in this story?
2. How does religion influence the world view of the people, organizations, or governments involved?
3. How is religion being used by politicians, leaders, and other individuals?
4. How is religion acting in a political capacity?
5. How is religion carrying out its religious mandates?

7

Comparing and Contrasting Religious Traditions

I t isn't often we get to see an idea that was rejected by one religious tradition played out to its logical extension in another tradition. But when we consider Jainism[1] with its apparent "salvation by good works" theme, that is what Christians see happening. Or is it?

The apostle Paul preached against the dangers of belief in salvation by works so strongly in his letters to early Christian churches that the prospects of Christianity ever becoming a tradition that admitted the possibility of self-won salvation seemed dim. Although the question of salvation by human energies did press itself on the church at several points,[2] works, in the end, have always played a subservient role to the twin engines of God-initiated grace and faith. Christians don't earn their salvation, God gives it to them.

Yet Christians do have a responsive role to God's gift of grace. Because that response involves displaying the fruits of the spirit (acting ethically), the questions of just how important that role is result in the question of merited salvation always being a part of Christian theological consideration. Christians are often left wondering what Christianity would have looked like had the Judaizers won the day in the early church and mandated that following the law, the Christianized Jewish law, was necessary for salvation to be achieved. How, in the long run, would that have affected Christians' view of Jesus and his crucifixion?

Thus, when we read about how Mahavira, the founder of Jainism, developed his egalitarian reaction to the Brahmanic sacrificial system, a reaction that insisted that liberation came not from appropriate sacrifices but from an extremely rigorous practice of *ahimsa*, or nonviolence to any living creatures, we suddenly see a path to "salvation" that relies totally on individual effort. Mahavira taught that each person has a soul that bad karma sticks to like glass windows become dirty. Souls could be cleansed only through eliminating life-denying actions. The more rigorous the practice of *ahimsa*, the cleaner the soul. No god helps with this cleansing process. It is totally up to the individual.

There is an almost irresistible temptation for someone who knows the history of Christian thought on this subject and then reads about the Jain teaching, to compare the two. The student of religion is constantly faced with the possibility of such comparisons on a plethora of subjects. The world religions cover similar topics and often advocate similar answers to life's problems. Does that mean all religions are the same, at least on those points where they seem similar? Does that mean that some religions have better answers than others on these questions? What role should comparison have in our study of religion?

Compare and Contrast

At its most basic level, comparison is an unavoidable part of our thinking process. We define things we see and read about based on comparison. We know a horse and a cow are both the same and different because we compare them. They are similar in many ways: both are warm-blooded, four-footed, and hairy. Because of these and other significant similarities, we call them both mammals. They are also different in many obvious ways.

In religious studies, comparison can be used to similar advantage. In fact, early in the history of the study of religion, the discipline itself was called comparative religion.[3] At first, comparison was done mainly between the major religions themselves. In the late nineteenth century scholars were looking particularly hard at the so-called beginnings of all religions, and it was quite common for the search to involve a close look at how religions had evolved over their history to try to trace them back to a common root. This search eventually was abandoned when research showed that there was no common, universal root; the religions all had their own historical and mythological beginnings, similar in some ways, but quite unique in others.[4]

Although the search for common beginnings was abandoned, the use of comparison was not. It was soon applied not just to comparison between religions, but to the study of religion, that is, the common experience of human beings in their attempts to relate to the divine. Led by great scholars such as Gerardus van der Leeuw and Mircea Eliade, the phenomena of religion, the practices, rituals, and beliefs, became objects of study in their own right.[5] For example, the religious practice of prayer was studied in each of the major religious traditions. Researchers discovered that prayer is a feature common to almost all religions, but that its goals, forms, and functions might vary widely from religion to religion.[6] Almost all people pray (98 percent in the United States, the polls tell us) but there are many different ways to do it.

Comparison has a long and fruitful history in the study of religion. Unfortunately, it has almost as long a record of abuse.

As a research method, it has been stretched to justify several serious errors that have threatened the integrity of both the theological and academic study of religion.

The Dangers of Comparison

We have already seen one of the tempting misuses of comparison in the attempts of E. B. Tylor and R. R. Marett, both anthropologists, to isolate a common root to all religions. The mistake many of these scholars made was the *error of extrapolation.* The student of religion discovers amazing similarities between historically unrelated religions. Some of these commonalities can be traced to human nature—all human beings throughout history have been religious to some degree. Because we are made the same way (we are *homo sapiens*) our individual searches are likely to turn up similar answers to the ultimate questions that religion addresses: Who am I? What am I doing here? Where am I going? But for reasons we shall see shortly, it is a mistake to push too quickly to the conclusion that these similarities mean all religions are the same, or even that they came from the same philosophical, psychological, or sociological root. Careful research shows over and over again that the search for one world religion based on the common human thirst for the spiritual is sure to stumble over cultural, ethnic, and linguistic differences. The search also treats too cavalierly the deeply held belief of most religious people that their own religion is uniquely true.

To guard against the error of extrapolation, scholars doing comparative work always insist on using the phrase *compare and contrast*—that is, in every similarity it is likely there is also a difference. To use our earlier example, all people pray, but all do it differently from one another. A careful comparison lists both the similarities in prayer postures, content, and goals and the differences in prayer postures, content, and goals, and draws conclusions from both lists.

A second error is the *error of ahistoricism*. Religions change. Every tradition has a history, and that history often shows radical adjustments in many phases of its practice, sometimes even in its beliefs. A valid comparison must take into account the period of history the comparisons are drawn from. Am I studying something early in the religion's history? Late? What issues was the religious community struggling with at this time?

Although we must avoid the error of evolutionary thinking discussed previously, there is good evidence that religions do go through some common phases as they grow older. Sociologist Robert Bellah has described five stages that religions go through (primitive, archaic, historic, pre-modern, and modern).[7] Bellah takes great pains to point out that he is not saying that this increasing complexity in structure and form represents progress or improvement. He simply asserts that time produces increasingly complex societies and institutions that usually give greater freedom and choice to individuals, and that religions change in response to that.

A third error is the *error of identification*. When the student of religion finds a phenomenon in two different religions, the temptation is to too quickly identify the two as the same. Often the culprit here is translation of terms from one language to another. Early translations of Hindu texts into English used the Christian term *salvation* as the equivalent of the Hindu concept of *moksha*. There is some functional equivalence between the two: both describe the goal of achievement after the process of compliance with the divine mandates. But because the phenomena themselves have important differences, it is misleading to translate *moksha* by the term *salvation*. "Release" or "liberation" is a better choice (although now *liberation* is taking on a technical meaning within Christian theology that is making it, too, an inappropriate translation).

It is better to think of similar concepts in different religions in terms of analogies rather than identification. Saying one concept is analogous to another signals the kind of tentative compare-and-contrast relationship we are looking for.

A fourth error, the *error of triumphalism*, characterized much of the early Christian writing about other religions. Unfortunately, it is not altogether gone from the writings of modern religionists. Comparisons can be used to put down other religions as inadequate; comparisons can also be used to idealize other religions and put one's own down. Both are inappropriate uses of the technique.

Sometimes the abuse is flagrant and gross. Descriptions of the shortcomings of Muhammad, the founder of Islam, are a case in point. It is often pointed out that Muhammad was illiterate, had numerous wives, and was politically clever. These statements may all be true, but how one then uses this information can be devastating, as this quotation from Alexander Ross in 1696 illustrates: "Christianity exceeds Mahometanism as Jesus exceeds Mahomet. The one teaching love, peace and patience, the other hatred, war and revenge; the one curbing men's lust by monogamy, the other letting loose the reins to uncleanliness by Polygamy; the one working by miracles, the other by cheating tricks."[8]

Sometimes a value-laden comparison is a bit more refined. James Freeman Clarke wrote a widely used textbook in the nineteenth century called *Ten Great Religions*, in which he took the position that Christianity was better than all the rest of the world's religions, but only by degrees.[9]

A more common form of the error of triumphalism in recent years is for Western authors to put down their own religious tradition in favor of Eastern ones. The infamous Inquisition, for example, is often used as an example that typifies Christianity, instead of being described as an aberration of it. Laurette Sejourne corrects a similar misconception of Toltec/Aztec religion as an inhuman religion of human sacrifice, instead of describing it as a series of disastrous political and economic decisions that distorted the true religion of Quetzalcoatl.[10]

All such self-serving justifications and distortions are inappropriate uses of comparative technique. There is a place for evaluating religions on any one of several different scales. But evaluation must always be done fairly, long after the collective work of comparison and description is completed. In the next chapter we will look at how some of that work is done. For now, however, it is appropriate to look at some of the more immediate benefits of comparing and contrasting.

The Benefits of Comparison

It may appear that we are dealing here with a highly explosive technique, one we might be better off doing without. But that would be a mistake. Many positive things happen when one compares and contrasts in proper balance and with clearly stated objectives.

One benefit is that comparison sharpens understandings. "Iron sharpens iron" the Bible says. As demonstrated by the seven steps suggested in the next section, comparison does not allow for any slippage in understanding either of the two sides being compared. If there is fuzziness, it will become quickly evident.

A second, related benefit is a deeper understanding of one's own religion as a whole. The father of modern religious studies, Max Müller, said that "he who knows one [religion] knows none."[11] The interplay between elements of different religious traditions leads to deeper understandings of what is unique to the religion on which one is an expert—or grew up in.

Finally, the fuller and richer the picture one gets of traditions on both sides of a comparison the more questions one is led to and the more areas one finds that need deeper exploration.[12] For instance, the comparison between Jainism and Christianity with which we led off this chapter can, in fact, be done profitably, as we shall soon see. The project is full of dangers and pitfalls, but the rewards of the comparison make it eminently worthwhile. What is needed is a road map to follow, a guide in how to make the comparison.

Follow These Seven Steps

1. *State the comparison.* Write down in simple language what it is you want to do. "I want to compare the Sikh concept of True Name with the Christian concept of God." Several features of these two concepts make this a promising comparison. Both gods have the same primitive Semitic desert origin in the God of Abraham. Thus, the gods are not original to either tradition. In addition, the basic nature of the God of Abraham was accepted by Sikhism via Islam and was recognized by Christians as the Father of Jesus Christ from Judaism.

2. *Develop a hypothesis.* As with all scientific work, it is easier to make a detailed study if one formulates a hypothesis to prove or disprove about the comparison. Great care must be taken to ensure that the hypothesis is not pejorative, that is, that it doesn't cast the comparison into the error of triumphalism. Part of its purpose is to limit a project. For example, a hypothesis regarding the Sikh/Christian comparison might be: "Although a common origin and many similarities exist between the Sikh and Christian conceptions of deity, the distinctive difference is the trinitarian nature of the Christian God."[13]

Your hypothesis does not need to exhaust the issue; it does not even need to be something you feel you must prove true. Much can be learned by disproving a hypothesis. But it does provide an anchor from which to work, and this is a necessity when dealing with enormously broad religious and cultural phenomena.

3. *Clarify the content.* Describe as clearly as possible the content of the two elements of your comparison. For example, if we are comparing the Sikh and Christian views of deity, we need to

state the Christian doctrine of God succinctly and clearly, and then do the same with the Sikh concept of True Name. This step is more than a formal exercise. It forces the student/scholar to understand clearly—well enough to write down in accurate summary form—both sides of the comparison.

Establish the context. Elements of any religion need to be understood in relation to existing sociological, economic, political, and religious conditions. Ask, for example, if the religious element being studied developed in opposition to an existing social, economic, or theological condition. The teachings of the Buddha arose, for example, in a particular area of India in the sixth century B.C.E. because what the Buddha was advocating (an egalitarian, individual-based path to freedom) corresponded well to a widespread dissatisfaction with the Hindu Brahmanical system that focused overmuch on expensive and elitist ritual sacrifice.[14]

Care must be taken that, in the process of looking for cultural, political, and economic factors in the rise of a religious teaching, one not denigrate or forget the element of truth in the teaching. What the Buddha taught had value simply because in some way (to whatever degree) it corresponded to the truth. No combination of contextual factors may be allowed to obscure that relationship.[15]

Analyze the function. Sometimes elements of one religious system, when described linguistically, can seem very similar to elements in other systems; similarities may or may not really exist depending upon the roles the elements play in their respective religions. One example of this, cited by philosopher Surjit Singh, is Rudolf Otto's *India's Religion of Grace and Christianity.*[16] Otto argues that even though "salvation" is the key and innermost phenomenon in both Christianity and Bhakti Hinduism, it plays a different role in each religion.

The similarities are startling: both religions have a concept of a personal God, both see humanity as separated from that God (albeit for different reasons), and both say adherents receive help from that God. But the differences are equally startling, especially the difference between the slow, gradual evolution of the Bhakti Hindu from "non-being to being, from darkness to light, from death to superdeath," and the sudden demands (and freely given gift) of holiness in the Christian tradition. When a careful look at the function of salvation is taken, the close identity of this "salvation" in the two traditions becomes merely an interesting analogy on one level and a clear distinction on another.

Locate it within the total system. Not only must the elements of the comparison be seen in light of the role they play in a religious system, but they must be evaluated on the relative importance of each in their respective systems. Both Mormons and Christians talk about salvation and mean much the same thing by it: the condition to which believers have access because of Jesus Christ's atoning death. But whereas for Christians salvation is the *sine qua non* of the religious life, the most important thing, for Mormons it is simply one step (which almost everyone attains) toward achieving a much higher state called exaltation.[17] Severe misunderstandings can result if the doctrine's relative importance in the total religious system is not taken into account.

Draw conclusions. The conclusion of your comparison should start with a clear statement of whether or not you have proved your hypothesis. This, of course, should be followed by your reasons for coming to that conclusion. As mentioned earlier, it is not crucial that you prove your hypothesis; what is important, however, is that your reasons for proof or disproof are clearly, logically stated and are backed up by good scholarly analysis and documentation.

Almost always, a comparison leads to increased, deepened understandings of the religious elements on both sides of the comparison. Christians comparing their doctrine of God with the Sikh True Name invariably find they discover a new facet to their own understanding of God. Buddhists forced to study the roots of their own tradition as deeply embedded in Hinduism see a new richness to their heritage. These deepened insights need to be fully articulated in the conclusion of your study.

One final element should be added to your concluding comments: questions that have arisen that demand further study. In any comparison, something is usually left unresolved. This should not be seen necessarily as indicating failure or incompleteness of the study, but as an exciting spur to further research or another comparison. The linkages are endless.

An Example

We are now ready to consider the questions we would have to deal with were we to carry out the *comparison* used to open this chapter—that of the Jain conception of "salvation by good works" and the largely discarded Christian notion of "salvation by works."

Our *hypothesis* might be the following: The Christian concern with faith and good works came at least in part from an effort to differentiate itself from Judaism, while the Jain teaching was an attempt to assert its independence from the Hindu Brahmanical sacrificial cult.

We described the *content* of the Jain teaching earlier. The Christian teaching is usually rooted in the apostle Paul's letters, particularly Titus 3:5, 1 Timothy 1:15, and Romans 2:1–16. The letter of James (2:18) must also be considered. Paul's teaching was this: if a person lived a perfect life, he or she could be saved by works. No one can, however, so only by faith can we be saved, by accepting the freely given gift of salvation God offers. God makes sinners righteous, and they thus do works representative of their new status.

Two important *contexts* must be considered in order to understand the Christian teaching. One is the biblical context. Some in the early Christian church thought salvation could still come through following the Jewish law, as enriched by Jesus' teaching. Most of Paul's teaching on the matter must be understood within this framework. The second is the historical context of the Protestant Reformation and the Roman Catholic Council of Trent. In general, the Roman Catholic Church allowed more of a place in the salvation process for good works than the newly established Protestant churches did. Both, however, taught that human beings must somehow be empowered by faith to be saved.

The appropriate Jain context would be Mahavira's reaction against the sacrificial system of the Hindus that made Enlightenment something much easier for the rich and privileged to obtain than for the poor. Mahavira rejected the expensive sacrifices that had to be made as unnecessary and ostentatious. He put the Path on a level that anyone could grasp; the only requirement was a will to live the life of total nonviolence, thereby eradicating the polluting effects of desire and the input of the senses.

Good works *function* in Christianity simply as signs that God has done the work of justification in one's life. "By their fruits you will know them," is the biblical Christian phrase. For the Jains, however, works and deeds are the sole factor in determining a person's religious status. "Good deeds" cleanse the soul. Without them, there is no hope.

Therefore, in the total system, works play a more important part in Jainism than in Christianity.

In *conclusion*, we could probably come close to proving our thesis. An interesting extension of the study would be to compare the Jain doctrine with the role of works in Judaism. One might be curious about how close the Jewish view of the importance of doing God's will as expressed in Torah is to the Jain view of soul purgation.

Each of the steps of this comparison needs to be expanded in great detail, of course. But this would be the outline one would follow. As you can see, the areas of religion in which this kind of work can be done are endless. And great profit is the result.

EXERCISES

If you are a Christian church member, compare the way your church baptizes believers with the way either the Baptist or the Presbyterian or another church down the street does it.

Compare the Christian notion of repaying evil with good with the Confucian notion of repaying evil with justice.

Part **3**

Explaining

8

The Questions of Truth, Value, and Effectiveness

We were studying Jainism, the Indian religion of good works mentioned in the last chapter, when one of my students raised her hand. "I think Jains are inconsistent," she offered. "They teach that those beings with more physical senses (such as taste, seeing, and so forth) are better off in life, yet they teach that the goal of religious life is to reduce the negative accumulations of sense impressions. I would think that according to such thinking, one-sense amoebas would be better off than you and I with our six senses."

Good comment. Belinda was really thinking and was processing the material. Whether or not she was correctly interpreting Jainism (or my explanation of it!) is a question I would like to tackle another day. What I would like to tackle in this chapter, however, is the nature of Belinda's comment: It was an evaluation. She was not asking for more primary infor-

mation, unless that was needed to correct any misunder-
standing her comment reflected of the basic teachings of Jainism. She was asking for and making a judgment. She was crit-
ically analyzing the religion that four million people in India
hold to be the truth.

Are religious studies scholars allowed to make judgments
about the religious traditions they study? This question gets
us into the complicated area of religious truth and value. It
sometimes appears that in an attempt to be fair, impartial, and
objective, scholars studiously avoid questions of valuation in
religious studies. In one sense that is true. Religion is such an
important part of people's lives that scholars want to avoid
either needlessly offending the people they are studying or
biasing their study by their own strong feelings. These dangers seem more acute in religious studies than in other disciplines. For some reason, philosophers can study idealism,
monism, realism, and naturalism and have far less chance of
offending idealists, monists, realists, and naturalists than religious studies scholars who study Buddhism, Hinduism, Christianity, Judaism, and Islam have of offending adherents of
those religious traditions.

Yet evaluation is an important part of religious studies. As
with any academic discipline, after the collecting of solid data
takes place and theories are developed about how the data
hangs together in coherent wholes, some judgments about
truth, value, and effectiveness are necessarily made. Special
precautions against the dangers must be taken in religious
studies, however.

My experience in teaching classes on the world's religions
is that students err in two basic ways when it comes to making evaluative judgments. Some zealously jump to comparing what they are learning with their own strongly held faith;
inappropriate judgments, sometimes intentional and sometimes unconscious, can be the result. This can quickly turn
the study of religion into an apologetic exercise in favor of

one religion over all the others. Apologetics in any religious tradition is an important endeavor, but it is not the primary work of the religious studies scholar.

On the other hand, in an attempt to avoid too quickly jumping to evaluation, some take the religious studies admonitions about respect for their subject matter to heart and extend those important feelings to unnecessary degrees. They abandon the search for truth altogether and become poorer scholars because of it.

Thus, it is ironic that in their attempts to avoid any unfair or inappropriate judgments, religious studies scholars argue a great deal over the very thing they try to be most careful about: the question of truth. Scholars argue about this issue even when the ultimate form of the question (Which religion is the true one?) is not an obvious part of the discussion. For philosophers, the question is usually stated this way: What is the nature of religious truth? Is religious truth the same as or different from scientific truth? How can anyone know religious truth?[1]

On the other hand, specialists in the study of religion— sociologists,[2] psychologists,[3] historians—usually attempt to phrase the question of truth in a different way. They deal more with questions of effectiveness. The sociologist of religion, for example, might say something like this: "I am interested in studying the effects of religious systems on human sociological systems (or vice versa). I am not making ultimate judgments about the truth of the religious systems, per se. I want to study how this religion works in this social setting." Effectiveness is the key standard. How does a religion work?

Insiders, like Christian theologians, confront the question of truth most directly. Because they start with theological presuppositions (such as, God exists, God is related somehow to human beings, and so forth), the question of the truth or falsity of other religions inheres in those presuppositions. As theologians attempt to work out the implications of their presuppositions, they usually take a stand on the question of what religious truth is.[4]

It already sounds complicated, doesn't it? As a budding scholar, you will need to know what measurements of truth and value other scholars are using when they do their work and write up their results. You will also have to decide what kind of evaluative standard you are going to use to apply to your work. It is important to realize that none of the standards we are going to describe in this chapter is necessarily right or wrong. As long as scholars are honest in describing their own standards, we are free to agree or disagree with those standards and also to measure the results of their work.

You may have noticed that I have not really defined the term *value*. This needs to be dealt with before we can say anything more about standards. Value means something a bit different from what is usually inferred by the word *truth* (or what's really out there). Value means something like "what is important to me (or us)." Why this distinction between value and truth? In order to understand, we need to take a brief look at the history of truth in our Western culture.

A Brief History of Religious Truth

Recent views of religious truth have swung between two emphases: an emphasis on the person seeking the truth, that is, the truth seeker and an emphasis on the truth to be known, or the content of truth. When I was a student in college, the following scenario was the topic of several long coffee-shop conversations: If a tree falls in the forest, does it make a noise even if there is no one there to hear the noise? We argued both sides of the question. But which conclusion we came to depended on how much we emphasized the importance of the fact that the tree fell (the content of truth) and how much we emphasized the presence of a truthseeker to hear the noise. Current discussions of truth have similar emphases, some stressing content more than the role of the truthseeker, others stressing the role of the seeker over the content of truth.

Traditionally in the history of Western philosophy and theology, the emphasis has been on the content of truth—the objective pole. Trees fall and crash, whether we are there to know about them or not. God exists and speaks, whether we recognize it or not. Truth is simply reality, and our role is to try, as precisely as possible, to identify and describe what is out there.[5]

But recent Western philosophy and theology have seen a renewed interest in the role of the truthseeker in defining what truth is. The reason for this is that focusing heavily on the content of truth has two major drawbacks when it comes to describing religious truth. The first is the problem of determining the nature of God or, in religions where God is absent, of the Transcendent. God is not a tree. When we try to describe the truth about God, we can only go part-way in our descriptions. We can say that God is like a king, God is good not evil, and God wants to help us. But we must admit that, in the end, there are some things about God we cannot describe, because God (or the Transcendent), by definition, lies outside the normal sphere of things that can be seen, heard, tasted, and felt. God eludes *final* description.

The second drawback is dealing with our own feelings about God. In most religions, but in Christianity especially, God or the Transcendent demands some kind of response from us. In Christianity this is called faith. Knowledge of God (truth) must start with a response on our part to God's attempts to reveal the divine nature to human beings. Augustine described this process as "faith seeking understanding."[6] Without this initial act of faith, the truth of God cannot be known in the fullest, religious sense of the word.

Western theologians and philosophers have tried to overcome these two drawbacks to theories of truth that emphasize the content end of the spectrum by devising systems of truth that emphasize the truthseeker end of the spectrum. Some have done this by saying that religious truth is different from scientific truth. If you are studying trees falling in the forest, then the old view of truth as facts that correspond to reality is fine. But if you are discussing God and religion, you must use a different standard for judging truth. Immanuel Kant developed the position that religious truth is not descriptive of reality but prescriptive of how we should behave.[7] Following Kant, Friedrich Schleiermacher provided the interpretation that religious truth is not descriptive of reality but expressive of how we feel.[8] Another standard was adopted by Søren Kierkegaard, who said that religious truth is not descriptive of reality but effective in connecting us with God.[9] If the language we use leads us to a better understanding of our essential relationship of faith in God, then it is judged effective religiously.

In the views of Kant, Schleiermacher, and Kierkegaard, whether or not religious stories correspond to reality in the scientific sense is beside the point. Religious stories should really be judged by whether or not they make us act ethically, make us feel truly human, or connect us with God. The standard is not the content of the stories, but our human reaction to them. The emphasis is not on the accuracy of a description of a tree falling in the forest, but on the appropriateness of the truthseeker's reaction to the tree falling in the forest. The emphasis cannot be on the accuracy of a description of God, because God cannot be finally described anyway. What is important is the nature of our response to God. The emphasis is not on truth in the empirical sense but on the value of a teaching or an action to us. This is called a subjective approach to truth.

Naturally, to demonstrate what is distinctive in this way of approaching truth, I have done a great deal of simplification. In practice, few religious scholars would claim to base their understanding of truth entirely on its content or entirely on the truthseeker. Most theories are a combination of the two approaches. One prominent scholar who has attempted to blend the two views is Wilfred Cantwell Smith.[10]

Over the past thirty years Smith has written a number of articles on the subject of religious truth. His major concern in them all is what he perceives to be an overemphasis in many religions on the content of truth. This is unfortunate, Smith says, because the kinds of truth statements and descriptions that focus on content are usually things that change over time (the history of a religion) or are doctrines and dogmas on which it is difficult to find agreement even within religious traditions, much less among several different religions. Further, no one of us is really an objective observer of religion anyway; we all bring our biases and preconceived notions to our observations, no matter how hard we try to control them. Thus, according to Smith, a much better place to look for religious truth is in "the faith in men's hearts." The "locus of truth is persons," he says, not creeds or histories of traditions. "Christianity, or any religion, is not true or false; they become true or false only as you or I appropriate them" and live them out. In the end, for Smith, religious truth is best judged by whether or not a person's religion brings him or her closer to God.

Smith does not dismiss the content end of religion entirely; he admits that the correspondence of religious doctrines to the way things really are is important. (This is often called the correspondence theory of truth.) Religious statements, to be valid, must correspond as far as we can know to the way things are in the world. But his point is that any measure of religious truth that neglects the motivation of the truth-seeker and the way that truth works its way out in the individual seeker's life will be incomplete and thus false.

Most critics of Smith say that he does, in fact, place undue emphasis on the role of the truthseeker in knowing truth and he tips the balance in that direction, just as Kant and Schleiermacher have done. Traditional theologians object that the correspondence theory of truth—liberally laced with good doses of humility and the willingness to say, "I don't know" at certain points—will serve us just fine. Usually they point out the dangers of either reducing religion to ethics or feelings, or overemphasizing the religious subject's role in determining truth. In doing any of these things, they say, the objective standards by which most religions measure truth (Holy Scriptures, God's appearances, divinely revealed systems of doctrine) are needlessly minimized or lost.

From my point of view, both truth and value are important to religious studies. Indeed, they seem to come together in religious studies as they do in no other area of life. Look at one definition of religious truth, offered by Frederick Streng: "Religious truth can be defined as the knowledge and expression of what-is for the purpose of achieving the greatest well-being possible (i.e., salvation, absolute freedom, or total harmony)."[11] In this definition both truth as the way things are and truth as what is most valuable for me are included.

From this brief history of religious truth in Western thought, you can see why some scholars distinguish between the evaluative words *truth* and *value*, sometimes reserving the former for science and the latter for religion. Other scholars don't make this distinction. Still others prefer not to talk about it at all, seeing the issues as lying outside the purview of religious studies per se. It is precisely because of these disagreements within the field itself that we must be carefully aware of what standard of evaluation scholars use. So let's look at some of the possibilities.

Defining Standards of Truth, Value, and Effectiveness

Identifying the standard of truth, value, or effectiveness used in any scholarly work means asking (and answering) three questions:

Is the intended judgment absolute or relative? Absolute standards of truth assert that something is true for all times and all places. Relative standards maintain that something is true for some times and some places but not for others. Most, if not all, of the world's religions recognize both absolute and relative truth standards. For Muslims, for example, the teachings of the Quran are absolute truth judgments, true for all times and places. The rules of an individual mosque on how its members should behave, however, are mostly relative truth standards, applicable only to the members of that mosque. It is true that other mosques may have similar rules; indeed, it is likely. But the variations between mosques are questions of relative truth, not absolute truth, except where they are specifically mandated by the teachings of the Quran. In most religions, the truths of God or the Transcendent tend to be seen as absolute, supported by the relative truths of institutional and ecclesiastical organizations.

Similarly, when religious studies scholars talk about truth, value, or effectiveness, they may sometimes be referring to these standards as absolute for all times and all places and at other times (and this is more often the case) be referring to them as relative, depending on a particular religion in a particular time and place. Thus, when speaking of truth in religions, we must make it clear whether we are talking about absolute or relative truth.

Is the scope of the judgment interreligious or intrareligious, that is, among different religions or within one religious tradition? It is extremely important to understand whether a judgment is based on the teachings of a single religion or whether it is meant to be a judgment that adopts a stance outside any particular religion and thus applies to all. It is possible, for example, to judge the truth of all religions against the teachings of Judaism and how Jews view God and the world. This is something that Jewish theologians have done and must do, just as

Christian theologians and Hindu and Buddhist philosophers do with respect to the teachings of their religious traditions.

But it is also possible to devise systems of truth and value that are intended for use across religious boundaries according to some standard that is not rooted in any one tradition, but is outside of or common to them all. For example, one could use personal spiritual satisfaction as the standard of truth or value for all religions: How effective is a religious tradition in satisfying human beings' spiritual urges? Of course, in order to use such a standard, one must either prove or assume that the standard is common to all people being measured (e.g., that all people have spiritual longings). And, like other standards, it must then be carefully defined in a way that lends itself to useful measurement.

What is the standard of truth or value? Different scholars use different standards against which to measure truth or value. Sometimes the standard is obvious. For example, if you are a judge in a strongest-man-in-the-world contest, you know that the participants will be judged on how much weight they can lift. This does not mean that this is the only standard against which the participants could be measured. The weakest contestant might be the fastest runner. But when the strength standard is used, he loses.

At other times the standard is not so obvious and must be spelled out clearly. For example, your daughter's school may give an award for being the best citizen of the school. The standard could be any one of several things (or all of them): good grades, participation in clubs, good deportment, faithful attendance. The important thing is that the standard be well defined.

In religious studies, sociologists of religion tend to measure religions by how well they contribute to the well-being of a culture or society. Psychologists of religion tend to measure them by how well they contribute to an integrated personality or a pathology-free personality. Philosophers measure religions by how well their belief systems stack up against standards of correspondence to reality or coherence. Theologians use internal standards unique to each of their systems: what sacred scriptures say, what the historical tradition has taught, what the cumulative experiences of the adherents describe. Some theologians, such as Ross Reat and Edmund Perry in *A World Theology: The Central Spiritual Reality of Humankind* (Cambridge: Cambridge University Press, 1991), are attempting to develop more inclusive standards. None of these standards of truth or value are necessarily right or wrong. In the same way that I can choose to measure the length of my desk with a ruler that is divided into inches, feet, and yards or one that is divided into centimeters and meters, so religious studies scholars have a variety of "rulers" at their disposal. But the measuring tool being used must be clearly stated, so that other scholars and researchers can evaluate the evaluations.

A Simplified Paradigm of Approaches to Religious Truth

An alternative to the content versus truthseeker division we used earlier to describe the current philosophical and theological discussions of truth is to think of theories of truth in terms of where the standards of truth are located in time. Some scholars find their standards against which to measure truth in the past; others find them in the present, still others in the future. Let's look briefly at examples of each.

The past. Some scholars evaluate religious truth claims by measuring them against standards they have accepted from the past. For example, it may be an authoritative Scripture that was written down, usually seen to have been revealed from God, that is the standard against which present-day beliefs and actions are measured. Or the mighty acts of God in history, all human history, may be the benchmarks against which modern-day events are evaluated. Or it may be a cumu-

lative tradition of a faith community over thousands of years
that has final authority for judging truth.

A good example of a tradition that uses the standard of
revealed Scripture to determine truth is modern American
evangelical Christianity. In an article entitled "The Biblical
Concept of Truth," evangelical scholar Roger Nicole closely
examines the words used for truth in both the Old and New
Testaments of the Bible and concludes from those usages that
the Christian concept of truth "is like a rope with several inter-
twined strands. . . . The full Bible concept of truth involves
factuality, faithfulness, and completeness." Evangelical Christians use the Bible as the final arbiter of truth, because they
believe the Bible is the revealed word of God. For them, it is
the standard against which everything in the world, Christian and non-Christian, is measured.[12]

In a slightly different way, some Hindus also use a standard from the past to measure truth. Dayananda Sarasvati,
the nineteenth-century founder of a Hindu reform movement called the Arya Samaj, considered the Vedas, the oldest
of the Hindu sacred scriptures, the authoritative standard
against which right-thinking Hindus should measure their
behavior. According to Dayananda, God is the creator first
of the Vedas and then of the world. Hence, the Vedas are eternal as compared with the world: "The Vedas exist in God. At
the beginning of creation the Lord propagated the Vedas."[13]
Just as there are various Christian ways of viewing the authority of the Bible, there are various Hindu ways of viewing the
Vedas as a standard. But some at least view them as the defining documents of Hindu truth.

Another example of a standard of truth from the past comes
from yet another religious tradition in another part of the
world. Confucianism teaches the Chinese a pattern of behavior in regard to elders, employers, kings, children, siblings,
husbands, and wives that hearkens back to the good old days,
a golden age when everything was more ordered and har-

monious than it is now. For centuries, the teachings of Confucius, collected in five major works, have been the basis of an ethical system that influences Chinese culture to this day. In one sense, some Confucianists raise the tradition of a long-past culture to the status of an absolute standard of truth.

The present. Some scholars, particularly those trained in the humanities and social sciences, use present-oriented standards of truth. Often these standards are recognized by those using them to be relative, temporary, and partial—measures of sociological and psychological health, for example. Others, however, view certain present-oriented standards as absolute, at least as far as we are able to understand them; philosophers, for example, look to measures of coherent systems of logical thought as the model against which religious belief systems should be evaluated.

An interesting standard that measures the sociological effectiveness of new religious movements is offered by Rodney Stark in "How New Religions Succeed: A Theoretical Model."[14] Stark suggests that new religious movements are likely to succeed over the long haul to the extent that they accomplish eight things: 1) retain cultural continuity with the conventional faiths of the societies in which they appear or originate; 2) maintain a medium level of tension with their surrounding environment; 3) achieve effective mobilization, strong governance, and a high level of individual commitment; 4) attract and maintain adherents who are representative of the surrounding population in the demographics of age and sex; a normal age and sex structure; 5) operate within a favorable ecology that is sustained when the religious economy is relatively unregulated; 6) maintain dense internal network relations without becoming isolated; 7) resist secularization; and 8) adequately socialize the young. Obviously, Stark is not commenting on the absolute truth of religions; he is interested in observing the sociological factors that appear to lead to a new religion's survival. Other sociologists might use different factors.

One example of a present-oriented evaluation system built on a philosophical analysis of all religions is John Hick's. For Hick, a religion is successful or not to the extent that it aids individuals in moving from self-centeredness to Reality-centeredness, where Reality is the ultimate reality toward which all religions point and offer "salvation" systems for attainment. The technique for refining and honing this standard is a "continuing dialogue [that] will prove to be a dialogue into truth and [will lead to] a fuller grasp of truth [so that] our present conflicting doctrines will ultimately be transcended."[15]

The future. Future-oriented standards of truth take seriously the view common to most theologians and religious studies scholars that the transcendent realm of all religions can be known only imperfectly in the present; thus our knowledge of it can be complete only in the future. Some scholars attempt to construct evaluative standards for measuring truth and value that highlight this belief.

Perhaps the most prominent of these scholars today is Wolfhart Pannenberg. As a Christian theologian, Pannenberg affirms the Christian tradition. But he believes Christianity must be provable by rational standards. This means proving the existence of God. But God, by all widely accepted definitions, is beyond our proving. So we must look for God through God's effect on the world. The one place where we can most easily see this effect is in the history of human efforts at religion. By what standard can we evaluate those efforts? By measuring them against the promises inherent in the life and teachings of Jesus Christ that will be fully understood only at some point in the future. So we must comprehend the truth of what Christ was preaching and teaching as realizable only in the future and must allow our evaluations to be guided by that future, unified state.[16]

Another approach to a future-oriented truth standard is taken by Raimundo Panikkar. Panikkar argues that growth is an indispensable element of all religion: "The future, hope, eschatology, [and] the end of man, life, and the world are fundamental religious categories. Religion is essentially inclined towards the future."[17] We should expect growth in religions, says Panikkar, and in evaluating or judging any religion, growth is an important, perhaps the most important, standard.

There are many other standards that religious studies scholars use to measure truth, value, and effectiveness. Our short list is just a sampling. We should neither exaggerate the importance of the differences between them nor distinguish too sharply among them. Although scholars do start from different points and do use different strategies, the best religious studies scholars recognize that many standards have relative value. Even if absolute standards are being attempted, within those larger parameters the work of scholars using more restricted standards is indispensable.

EXERCISE

Read articles from at least seven different religious studies journals, and identify the truth, value, or effectiveness standards that the author of each article seems to be using by answering the three questions about absoluteness versus relativity, scope, and standards that are raised on pages 120–23.

Ask who and what the authors seem to cite most as their authorities.

Decide whether their standards are based in the past, present, or future.

Select journals from the following: History of Religions, Journal for the Scientific Study of Religion, Journal of the American Academy of Religion, Journal of Religion, Numen, Parabola, Religion and American Culture, Religion and Public Education, Religious Studies, *and* Review of Religious Research.

9

Doing Further Research

I f you have faithfully done the eight exercises in this book, you now have a taste for what it means to do religious studies research. You have touched the major issues of research that religious studies scholars face and have perhaps even struggled with some of the implications of them yourself. No doubt, some of the exercises were at least a bit disconcerting. I hope the taste of religious studies has been sweet. If so, stick with it, and I predict you will not only develop your religious studies skills but will have your personal faith deepened.

You have not arrived yet, however. The field is vast, and even if you have started to get an inkling of how you might want to focus your interests, you still need to look at religious studies as an ongoing, neverending task. I do not use the word *neverending* in the sense of tedious, because religious people never fail to change, surprise, and challenge. I mean neverending in the sense that there is so much to learn—there are so many church naves to poke into, forest firewalking rituals to observe, and charismatic religious leaders to interview. So you must now develop a plan for continued study.

Actually, if you are in school and are taking classes, your research capacities should be challenged continually. But you may not be in school—and, at any rate, you won't be there forever. You may want to continue doing religious studies as an avocation rather than as a profession. So developing a mindset now that will dovetail with your specialized interests is important. In the next few paragraphs I want to suggest strategies for continuing to do religious studies research—even when you aren't.

The Arts

As you read novels, attend plays, and listen to music, never forget that some of the most powerful themes in the history of art have been religious ones. Identify those themes when they are obvious and dig for them when they are not. Four years ago I toured the famous Hermitage Art Museum in St. Petersburg (then Leningrad), Russia. Massive oil canvases covered the walls, works that depicted Christian religious scenes. All this stupendous art was carefully preserved by an avowedly atheist government. Is it any wonder that when Marxism fell there in 1989 the church in Russia proved to be so vital—even after seventy years of relentless persecution?

One of my favorite novels is *The Count of Monte Cristo* by Alexandre Dumas. I have read and reread it numerous times over the years. Only in the past few years, though, have I focused on its basic theme, the relentless pursuit of revenge, from a primarily theological viewpoint. Looking at it in this way has added a great deal of depth and texture to my appreciation of one of my favorite works and, in the process, has made me a better theologian.

Or consider movies. When watching a film, try to identify its underlying value system and locate it in religious time and space, if possible. Great films stand out because they articulate a consistent world view in a true-to-life setting. Identifying each writer's or director's world view can be an excellent exercise in deepening your awareness of the many links between culture, the arts, and religion.

Mass Media

One of the exercises in this book asks you to read the newspaper religiously. If you did this, you began to get a grasp of the crucial role religion plays in so many areas of our lives. Perhaps you also began to get a new sense of why people in different parts of the world behave so differently—and so similarly. Religious beliefs make a difference in the way people behave. Practice discerning those motivations where possible.

Don't limit yourself to the newspaper. Read magazines religiously; watch television religiously. The interplay between culture, religion, the mass media, and media personalities is endlessly fascinating and instructive.

People

Finally, view people with a religious eye. Public people are textbooks in religiously motivated behavior. Several years ago New York Democrats Mario Cuomo and Geraldine Ferraro adopted an interesting view of abortion: They were against it in private life and in favor of it in public life. This occasioned a great deal of discussion. In last year's election, George and Barbara Bush adopted equally interesting positions on abortion, both of them seeming to differ with each other and with the Republican Party platform. All of this, whatever your position on abortion, is valuable grist for the mill of the religion and politics cipher.

Muhammad Ali, who changed his name for religious reasons and went to jail to avoid fighting in the Vietnam War, is an example of a public person making expressions that reveal the influence of religious values on behavior. Other examples of this: college football halfbacks kneeling for prayer in the end zone after scoring a touchdown; basketball players crossing themselves at the free-throw line; South African athletes refusing to compete with black athletes—or being refused the right to do so because of their nation's racial policies.

You already realize that the people you know personally—friends, relatives, co-workers—work out their religion in everyday life, both consciously and unconsciously. And so do you. Be aware in these most intimate settings of the intricate religious connections between life and belief.

In short, there is no lack of opportunity for you to do "religious studies research" even when you are not. Take advantage of it. It will keep the scholarly juices flowing and will give you a lifetime of intriguing thinking as you yourself figure out and deepen the religious rhythms of your life.

Appendix

Checklist for a Religious Studies Project

1. My definition of religion for this project is:

2. I am primarily adopting the role of:

    ___Theologian/Insider
    ___Reporter
    ___Specialist

If reporter or specialist, the following word best captures my role:

___Anthropologist	___Archaeologist
___Comparativist	___Historian
___Mythologist	___Phenomenologist
___Philosopher	___Psychologist
___Sociologist	___Other (Specify)

3. My field of inquiry is bounded in time, space, and structure:

Time
    1) Dates:

2) Key characteristics of this time period:

3) Relationships of this period to other periods in the tradition:

Space

1) Influence of religion on culture:

2) Influence of culture on religion:

3) History of the various relationships between culture and religion:

Structure

1) Role of this practice or belief within religious tradition:

2) Role of this practice or belief across traditions:

4. I will need to use the following research techniques for my project:

___Interviews
___Observation
___Participants' observations
___Written surveys
___None of the above

Resource people to interview or observe include:

    ___Experts:

    ___Practitioners:

    ___ The nonreligious:

5. Steps I will take to avoid bias, both mine and others, in my research project:

6. I will need to analyze the relationships between religion and culture in the setting of this project.

    ___Yes

    ___No

If yes, here is a brief description of how I will do that:

7. Comparing and contrasting religious beliefs and practices will be necessary to my study.

    ___Yes

    ___No

If yes, here is a brief outline of how I will arrive at the following elements of the comparison:

Hypothesis:

Content:

Context:

Function:

Importance in the total system:

8. The word that best describes my evaluative standard is:

    ___Truth
    ___Value
    ___Effectiveness

My evaluative standard could also be described as:

    ___Past
    ___Present
    ___Future

My standard of truth is:

    ___Absolute
    ___Relative

The scope of my standard is:

    ___Interreligious
    ___Intrareligious

My standard of truth or value can be described more fully as:

Select Bibliography

Adler, Mortimer. *Truth in Religion: The Plurality of Religions and the Unity of Truth.* New York: Macmillan, 1990.

Allport, Gordon W. *The Individual and His Religion: A Psychological Interpretation.* New York: Macmillan, 1961.

Anderson, J. N. D. *Christianity and World Religions.* Downers Grove, Ill.: InterVarsity, 1984.

Augustine. *Of True Religion.* J. H. S. Burleigh, trans. Chicago: Regnery, 1959.

Baird, Robert D. *Category Formation and the History of Religions.* The Hague: Mouton, 1971.

Banton, Michael, ed. *Anthropological Approaches to the Study of Religion.* Conference on New Approaches in Social Anthropology. London: Tavistock, 1968.

Bellah, Robert N. *Beyond Belief: Essays on Religion in a Post-Traditional World.* New York: Harper and Row, 1970.

Berger, Peter L. *The Sacred Canopy: Elements of a Sociological Theory of Religion.* Garden City, N.Y.: Doubleday, 1967.

Bettis, Joseph D. *Phenomenology of Religion: Eight Modern Descriptions of the Essence of Religion.* New York: Harper and Row, 1969.

Bianchi, Ugo. *The History of Religions.* Leiden: Brill, 1975.

Bleeker, Claas Jouco. *The Sacred Bridge.* Leiden: Brill, 1963.

Bolich, Gregory G., Byron R. Care, and Garrett Kenney. *Introduction to Religion.* Dubuque, Iowa: Kendall-Hunt, 1988.

137

Bouquet, Alan Coates. *Comparative Religion*. 7th ed. Baltimore: Penguin, 1967.

Brandon, S. G. F. *Time and Mankind*. London: Hutchinson, 1951.

Campbell, Joseph. *The Hero with a Thousand Faces*. Princeton: Princeton University Press, 1949.

Capps, Walter H. *Ways of Understanding Religion*. New York: Macmillan, 1972.

Carmody, Denise L., and John T. Carmody. *Ways to the Center: An Introduction to World Religions*. Belmont, Calif.: Wadsworth, 1989.

Chantepie de la Saussaye, Pierre D. *Manual of the Science of Religion*. New York: Longmans, Green, 1891.

Clark, W. H. *The Psychology of Religion: An Introduction to Religious Experience and Behavior*. New York: Macmillan, 1958.

Coleridge, Samuel. *Confessions of an Inquiring Spirit*. Menston, England: Scolar, 1971.

Comstock, W. Richard. *The Study of Religion and Primitive Religions*. New York: Harper and Row, 1972.

Douglas, Mary. *Natural Symbols: Explorations in Cosmology*. New York: Pantheon, 1970.

Durkheim, Emile. *The Elementary Forms of the Religious Life*. New York: Macmillan, 1915.

Eliade, Mircea. *Patterns in Comparative Religion*. Rosemary Sheed, trans. New York: World, 1963.

Eliade, Mircea. *The Sacred and the Profane: The Nature of Religion*. Willard R. Trask, trans. New York: Harcourt, Brace, 1959.

Eliade, Mircea, and Joseph Kitagawa, eds. *The History of Religions: Essays in Methodology*. Chicago: University of Chicago Press, 1959.

Ellwood, Robert S., Jr. *Many Peoples, Many Faiths: An Introduction to the Religious Life of Humankind*. Englewood Cliffs, N.J.: Prentice-Hall, 1982.

Evans-Pritchard, E. E. *Theories of Primitive Religion*. Oxford: Clarendon, 1965.

Feuerbach, Ludwig. *The Essence of Christianity* George Eliot, trans. New York: Harper, 1957.

Frazer, James George, Sir. *The Golden Bough: A Study in Magic and Religion*. New York: Macmillan, 1922.

Freud, Sigmund. *The Future of an Illusion*. Garden City, N.Y.: Doubleday, 1964.

Fromm, Erich. *The Dogma of Christ, and other Essays on Religion, Psychology, and Culture*. Garden City, N.Y.: Doubleday, 1963.

Geertz, Clifford. *The Interpretation of Cultures: Selected Essays*. New York: Basic, 1973.

Hall, T. William, ed. *Introduction to the Study of Religion*. San Francisco: Harper and Row, 1978.

Hart, Ray L., ed. *Trajectories in the Study of Religion*. Addresses at the Seventy-fifth Anniversary of the American Academy of Religion. Atlanta: Scholars, 1987.

Haught, John F. *What Is Religion?* New York: Paulist, 1990.

Heiler, Friedrich. *Erscheinungsformen und Wesen der Religion*. Stuttgart: W. Kohlhammer, 1961.

Hick, John. *An Interpretation of Religion: Human Responses to the Transcendent*. New Haven: Yale University Press, 1989.

Honko, Lauri, ed. *Science of Religion: Studies in Methodology*. Proceedings of the Study Conference of the International Association for the History of Religions. The Hague: Mouton, 1979.

Hopfe, Lewis M. *Religions of the World*. New York: Macmillan, 1987.

Howkins, Kenneth G. *The Challenge of Religious Studies*. Downers Grove, Ill.: InterVarsity, 1972.

Howkstra, Dennis, and Arnold H. De Graaff. *Contrasting Christian Approaches to Teaching Religion and Biblical Studies*. Grand Rapids: Calvin College, 1973.

Hume, David. *Dialogues Concerning Natural Religion*. New York: Hafner, 1948.

James, E. O. *Prehistoric Religion*. New York: Barnes and Noble, 1961.

James, William. *The Varieties of Religious Experience: A Study in Human Nature*. New York: Mentor, 1958.

Jastrow, Morris, Jr. *The Study of Religion*. New York: Scribners, 1990.

Jung, Carl Gustav. *Modern Man in Search of a Soul*. New York: Harcourt, Brace, 1933.

Jung, Carl Gustav. *Psychology and Religion*. New Haven: Yale University Press, 1938.

Karsten, Rafael. *The Origins of Religion*. London: Kegan, Paul, Trench, Trubner, 1935.

Kierkegaard, Søren. *The Present Age, and Of the Difference between a Genius and an Apostle*. Alexander Dru, trans. New York: Harper and Row, 1962.

King, Winston L. *Introduction to Religion: A Phenomenological Approach*. New York: Harper and Row, 1968.

Kitagawa, Joseph M. *The History of Religions Understanding Human Experience*. Atlanta: Scholars, 1987.

Kolakowski, Leszek. *Religion, If There Is No God*. New York: Oxford University Press, 1982.

Kraemer, Hendrik. *Religion and the Christian Faith*. Philadelphia: Westminster, 1957.

Kristensen, William Brede. *The Meaning of Religion*. The Hague: Martinus Nijhoff, 1968.

Lang, Andrew. *The Making of Religion*. New York: AMS, 1968, reprint of the 1898 ed.

Leach, Edmund, ed. *The Structural Study of Myth and Totemism*. London: Tavistock, 1967.

Leeuw, Gerardus van der. *Religion in Essence and Manifestation*. 2 vols. J. E. Turner, trans. New York: Harper and Row, 1963.

Lessa, William A., and Evon Z. Vogt, eds. *Reader in Comparative Religion: An Anthropological Approach*. New York: Harper and Row, 1979.

Lessing, Gotthold Ephraim. *Theological Writings*. Stanford: Stanford University Press, 1956.

Levi-Strauss, Claude. *The Savage Mind*. Chicago: University of Chicago Press, 1966.

Levy-Bruhl, Lucien. *How Natives Think*. Lilian A. Clare, trans. Princeton: Princeton University Press, 1985.

Lewis, James F., and Williams G. Travis. *Religious Traditions of the World*. Grand Rapids: Zondervan, 1991.

Livingston, James C. *Anatomy of the Sacred: An Introduction to Religion*. New York: Macmillan, 1989.

Lowie, Robert H. *Primitive Religion*. New York: Liveright, 1948.

Ludwig, Theodore M. *The Sacred Paths: Understanding the Religions of the World*. New York: Macmillan, 1989.

Malinowski, Bronislaw. *Magic, Science and Religion, and other Essays*. Garden City, N.Y.: Doubleday, 1948.

Marett, R. R. *The Raw Material of Religion*. Oxford: Oxford University Press, 1929.

Morris, Leon. *The Abolition of Religion*. Downers Grove, Ill.: InterVarsity, 1964.

Muck, Terry C. *Alien Gods on American Turf.* Wheaton, Ill.: Victor, 1990.

———. *Those Other Religions in Your Neighborhood.* Grand Rapids: Zondervan, 1992.

Müller, F. Max. *Introduction to the Science of Religion.* London: Longmans, Green, 1873.

Nakamura, Hajime. *Parallel Developments: A Comparative History of Ideas.* Ronald Burr, ed. Tokyo: Kodansha, 1975 (distributed by Harper and Row).

Nielsen, Niels C., et al. *Religions of the World.* New York: St. Martins, 1988.

Noss, David S., and John B. Noss. *A History of the World's Religions.* New York: Macmillan, 1990.

Nygren, Anders. *Essence of Christianity: Two Essays.* Philip S. Watson, trans. Grand Rapids: Eerdmans, 1960.

Otto, Rudolf. *The Idea of the Holy.* John W. Harvey, trans. London: Oxford University Press, 1923.

Paden, William E. *Religious Worlds: The Comparative Study of Religion.* Boston: Beacon, 1988.

Panikkar, Raimundo. *Myth, Faith, and Hermeneutics: Cross-Cultural Studies.* New York: Paulist, 1979.

Parrinder, Edward Geoffrey. *Comparative Religion.* London: Allen and Unwin, 1962.

Pettazzoni, Raffaele. *Essays on the History of Religions.* H. J. Rose, trans. Leiden: Brill, 1967.

Pratt, James Bissett. *The Psychology of Religious Belief.* New York: Macmillan, 1907.

Pruyser, Paul W. *A Dynamic Psychology of Religion.* New York: Harper and Row, 1968.

Pye, Michael. *Primitive Religion: An Introduction through Source Materials.* Newton Abbot: David and Charles, 1972.

Radin, Paul. *Comparative Religion: Its Nature and Origin.* New York: Dover, 1937.

Ramsey, Paul, and John F. Wilson, eds. *The Study of Religion in Colleges and Universities.* Princeton: Princeton University Press, 1970.

Ricoeur, Paul. *History and Truth.* Charles A Kelbley, trans. Evanston, Ill.: Northwestern University Press, 1965.

Robertson, Roland, ed. *Sociology of Religion: Selected Redings.* Baltimore: Penguin, 1969.

Robinson, Theodore H. *A Short Comparative History of Religions.* 2d ed. London: Duckworth, 1951.

Schleiermacher, Friedrich. *On Religion: Speeches to Its Cultured Despisers.* Richard Crouter, trans. Cambridge: Cambridge University Press, 1988.

Schmidt, Roger. *Exploring Religion.* Belmont, Calif.: Wadsworth, 1988.

Schmidt, Wilhelm. *The Origin and Growth of Religion.* H. J. Rose, trans. New York: Cooper Square, 1972.

Searles, Herbert. *The Study of Religion in State Universities.* Iowa City: University of Iowa, 1927.

Sharpe, Eric J. *Comparative Religion: A History.* LaSalle, Ill.: Open Court, 1986.

———. *Understanding Religion.* New York: St. Martin's, 1983.

Smart, Ninian, *The Religious Experience of Mankind.* 3d ed. New York: Scribner, 1984.

———. *The Science of Religion and the Sociology of Knowledge: Some Methodological Questions.* Princeton: Princeton University Press, 1973.

Smith, Wilfred Cantwell. *The Meaning and End of Religion: A New Approach to the Religious Traditions of Mankind.* New York: Macmillan, 1963.

Soderblom, Nathan. *The Living God.* London: Oxford University Press, 1933.

———. *The Nature of Revelation.* Frederic E. Pamp, trans. London: Oxford University Press, 1930.

Spencer, Herbert. *Principles of Sociology.* Abridged ed. Stanislav Andreski, ed. London: Macmillan, 1969.

Streng, Frederick J. *Understanding Religious Life.* Encino, Calif.: Dickenson, 1976.

Teilhard de Chardin, Pierre. *The Phenomenon of Man.* Bernard Wall, trans. New York: Harper and Row, 1959.

Tiele, C. P. *Elements of the Science of Religion.* New York: Scribners, 1899.

Tillich, Paul. *What Is Religion?* James Luther Adams, ed. New York: Harper and Row, 1969.

Toynbee, Arnold J. *An Historian's Approach to Religion.* 2d ed. Oxford: Oxford University Press, 1979.

Troeltsch, Ernst. *The Absoluteness of Christianity and the History of Religions.* David Reid, trans. Richmond, Va.: John Knox, 1971.

Turner, Victor W. *The Forest of Symbols: Aspects of Ndembu Ritual.* Ithaca, N. Y.: Cornell University Press, 1967.

Tylor, Edward Burnett. *Primitive Culture: Researches into the Development of Mythology, Philosophy, Religion, Language, Art, and Custom.* New York: Holt, 1889, repr. New York: Gordon, 1976.

van Baaren, Th. P., and H. J. W. Drijvers, eds. *Religion, Culture, and Methodology.* The Hague: Mouton, 1973.

Vries, Jan de. *Perspectives in the History of Religions.* Kees W. Bolle, trans. Berkeley: University of California Press, 1977.

Waardenburg, Jean Jacques. *Classical Approaches to the Study of Religion: Aims, Methods and Theories of Research.* The Hague: Mouton, 1973.

Wach, Joachim. *The Comparative Study of Religions.* New York: Columbia University Press, 1958.

―――. *Sociology of Religion.* Chicago: University of Chicago Press, 1953.

―――. *Types of Religious Experience, Christian and Non-Christian.* Chicago: University of Chicago Press, 1951.

Weber, Max. *The Sociology of Religion.* Ephraim Fischoff, trans. Boston: Beacon, 1963.

Welch, Claude. *Graduate Education in Religion: A Critical Appraisal.* Missoula, Mont.: University of Montana Press, 1971.

Whaling, Frank, ed. *Contemporary Approaches to the Study of Religion.* 2 vol. Berlin: Mouton, 1983–1984.

Whitehead, Alfred North. *Religion in the Making.* Lowell Lectures. New York: Macmillan, 1926.

Wiebe, Donald. *Religion and Truth: Towards an Alternative Paradigm for the Study of Religion.* The Hague: Mouton, 1981.

Wilson, Bryan R. *Religion in Secular Society.* Harmondsworth: Penguin, 1969.

Wilson, John Francis, and W. Royce Clark. *Religion: A Preface.* 2d ed. Englewood Cliffs, N.J.: Prentice-Hall, 1989.

Yinger, J. Milton. *The Scientific Study of Religion.* New York: Macmillan, 1970.

Endnotes

Introduction: Becoming a Student of Religion

1. There are many good world religion texts available for study. Among them, consider Gregory Bolich, Byron Care, and Garrett Kennery, *Introduction to Religion* (Dubuque, Iowa: Kendall-Hunt, 1988); A. C. Bouquet, *Comparative Religion*, 7th ed. (Baltimore: Penguin, 1967); Denise Carmody and John Carmody, *Ways to the Center: An Introduction to World Religions* (Belmont, Calif.: Wadsworth, 1989); Robert S. Ellwood, Jr., *Many Peoples, Many Faiths* (Englewood Cliffs, N.J.: Prentice-Hall, 1982); Lewis Hopfe, *Religions of the World* (New York: Macmillan, 1987); James Lewis and William Travis, *Religious Traditions of the World* (Grand Rapids: Zondervan, 1991); Theodore Ludwig, *The Sacred Paths* (New York: Macmillan, 1989); Niels Nielsen, et al., *Religions of the World* (New York: St. Martins, 1988); David Noss and John Noss, *A History of the World's Religions* (New York: Macmillan, 1990); Ninian Smart, *The Religious Experience of Mankind*, 3d ed. (New York: Scribner, 1984); Huston Smith, *The World's Religions* (New York: Harper, 1991).

2. There are many good methodological sources available, beginning with a history of the discipline, Eric Sharpe's *Comparative Religion: A History* (LaSalle, Ill.: Open Court, 1986). Sharpe's book and the bibliography in this book can point you to some of the early writings on methodology. Current books that go into more depth on the issues raised in this book include Robert Baird, *Category Formation, and the History of Religions* (The Hague: Mouton, 1971); Walter Capps, *Ways of Understanding Religion* (New York: Macmillan, 1972); Mircea Eliade and Joseph Kitagawa, eds., *The History of Religions: Essays in Methodology* (Chicago: University of Chicago Press, 1959); William Hall, ed., *Religion: An Introduction* (San Francisco: Harper and Row, 1985); John Haught, *What Is Religion?* (New York: Paulist, 1990); James Livingston, *Anatomy of the Sacred: An Introduction to Religion* (New York: Macmillan, 1989); William Paden, *Religious Worlds: The Comparative Study of Religion* (Boston: Beacon, 1988); Roger Schmidt, *Exploring Religion* (Belmont, Calif.: Wadsworth, 1988); Eric Sharpe, *Understanding Religion* (New York: St. Martin's, 1983); Frederick Streng, *Understanding Religious Life* (Encino, Calif.: Dickenson, 1976); John Francis Wilson and W. Royce Clark, *Religion: A Preface*, 2d ed. (Englewood Cliffs, N.J.: Prentice-Hall, 1989); J. Milton Yinger, *The Scientific Study of Religion* (New York:

145

Macmillan, 1970). For a historical study of religious studies complete with excerpts and full bibliographies, see Jean Jacques Waardenburg, *Classical Approaches to the Study of Religion* (The Hague: Mouton, 1973), and Frank Whaling, ed., *Contemporary Approaches to the Study of Religion*, 2 vols. (Berlin: Mouton, 1983–1984).

3. This complexity has also been the occasion for a great deal of discussion on just where the discipline of religious studies fits in higher education curriculums. A sampling of the literature: Stephen Crites, ed., *The Religion Major: A Report* (Atlanta: American Academy of Religion, 1990); Ray Hart, ed., *Trajectories in the Study of Religion* (Atlanta: Scholars, 1987); Dennis Howkstra and Arnold De Graaff, *Contrasting Christian Approaches to Teaching Religion and Biblical Studies* (Grand Rapids: Calvin College, 1973); Martin Marty, "What Is Modern about the Modern Study of Religion?" the University Lecture in Religion at Arizona State University (February 21, 1985); Jacob Neusner, "Stranger at Home: The Task of Religious Studies," Inaugural Lecture of the Department of Religious Studies at Arizona State University (October 25, 1979); Paul Ramsey and John F. Wilson, eds., *The Study of Religion in Colleges and Universities* (Princeton: Princeton University Press, 1970); Herbert Searles, *The Study of Religion in State Universities* (Iowa City: University of Iowa, 1927); Claude Welch, *Graduate Education in Religion: A Critical Appraisal* (Missoula, Mont.: University of Montana Press, 1971); and John F. Wilson and Thomas P. Slavens, *Research Guide to Religious Studies* (Chicago: American Library Association, 1982).

4. Books that raise some of the questions of faith and scholarship include J. N. D. Anderson, *Christianity and World Religions* (Downers Grove, Ill.: InterVarsity, 1984); Kenneth Howkins, *The Challenge of Religious Studies* (Downers Grove, Ill.: InterVarsity, 1972); Wilfred Cantwell Smith, *The Meaning and End of Religion* (New York: Macmillan, 1963); and Joachim Wach, *The Comparative Study of Religions* (New York: Columbia University Press, 1958).

Chapter 1: What Am I Observing?

1. Eric Sharpe, *Understanding Religion* (New York: St. Martin's, 1983), 47.

2. Morris Jastrow, Jr., *The Study of Religion* (New York: Scribners, 1909); C. P. Tiele, *Elements of the Science of Religion* (New York: Scribners, 1899); F. Max Müller, *Introduction to the Science of Religion* (London: Longmans, Green, 1873); G. W. F. Hegel, *Lectures on the Philosophy of Religion* (Berkeley: University of California Press, 1984); Mircea Eliade, *The Myth of the Eternal Return* (New York: Harper, 1959); and Fred Parrish, *The Classification of Religions* (Scottdale, Penn.: Herald, 1941).

3. Sharpe, *Understanding Religion*, 35.

4. I am not including in the three categories the so-called hostile definitions of religion that deny that there is anything to religion other than superstition, magic, neurosis, illness, or calculating self-interest. Proponents of these kinds of definitions include Sigmund Freud, who called religion an "illusion," and Karl Marx, who called it the "opiate of the people."

5. Friedrich Schleiermacher, *The Christian Faith* (Edinburgh: T & T Clark, 1989), 12.

6. William James, *The Varieties of Religious Experience* (New York: Mentor, 1958), 61.

7. Anders Nygren, *Essence of Christianity: Two Essays* (Grand Rapids: Eerdmans, 1960).

8. Rudolf Otto, *The Idea of the Holy* (London: Oxford University Press , 1923), 7, 12, 35.

9. Fuller discussion of these different approaches to religion will be added in later chapters.

10. Clifford Geertz, *Islam Observed* (New Haven: Yale University Press, 1968), 95–98.

11. John Hick, *An Interpretation of Religion* (New Haven: Yale University Press, 1989), 3–4.

12. Ludwig Wittgenstein, *Philosophical Investigations* (Oxford: Basil Blackwell, 1976), par. 66. Cited in Hick, *An Interpretation of Religion*.

13. James, *Varieties of Religious Experience*, 42.

14. Emile Durkheim, *The Elementary Forms of the Religious Life* (New York: Macmillan, 1915), 62.

Chapter 2: What Kind of Observer Am I?

1. David Noss and John Noss, *A History of the World's Religions* (New York: Macmillan, 1990), 444.

2. Ibid., 523.

3. The differences here are extremely important to the different religions.

4. For a good discussion of the differences between deductive and inductive methods in various academic disciplines, especially the ones related to the study of religion, see H. G. Hubbeling, "Theology, Philosophy and Science of Religion and Their Logical and Empirical Presuppositions" in Th. P. van Baaren and H. J. W. Drijvers, *Religion, Culture, and Methodology* (The Hague: Mouton, 1973), 9–35.

5. Recognizing that commitment is an indispensable element of a study that changes, for the better, the way the study is done, the results of the study, and the accuracy of the study, some scholars have tried to translate this element of commitment to the academic community. Unfortunately, this approach misses the precise element of religious commitment that needs to be understood—that it is commitment to the ultimate questions, not just relative ones. See T. William Hall, "Methodological Reflections," in T. William Hall, ed., *Religion: An Introduction* (San Francisco: Harper and Row, 1985), 250–63. See also Ninian Smart, *The Science of Religion and the Sociology of Knowledge* (Princeton: Princeton University Press, 1973), where he admits that religious explanations must come from both within a religious tradition (theology) and outside it (other disciplines). But by theology he seems to mean a kind of philosophical theology, not the committed theology of a believer. See pp. 110–34.

6. "Research for a Theological Faculty," *Theological Education* (Spring 1990): 86–106.

7. The Swedish Lutheran theologian Nathan Soderblom (1866–1931) was perhaps the best example of this historically. See *The Living God* (London: Oxford University Press, 1933) and *The Nature of Revelation* (London: Oxford University Press, 1930).

8. *The Comparative Study of Religions* (New York: Columbia University Press, 1958), 8.

9. *Essays on the History of Religions* (Leiden: Brill, 1967), 215.

10. Other examples of reductionists are the sociologists of knowledge who reduce all religious thought to sociological factors and, in the philosophical realm, the logical positivists who dismiss transcendent religious claims on linguistic bases.

11. Rudolf Otto, *The Idea of the Holy* (London: Oxford University Press, 1923), 8.

12. Joseph Campbell, *Hero with a Thousand Faces* (Princeton: Princeton University Press 1968); *Myths to Live By* (New York: Bantam, 1984).

13. John F. Haught, *What Is Religion?* (New York: Paulist, 1990), 11.

Chapter 3: What Does It Mean to Take Other Religions Seriously?

1. Wilfred Cantwell Smith, "The Comparative Study of Religion," McGill University divinity faculty inaugural lecture, 1949, excerpted in Walter Capps, *Ways of Understanding Religion* (New York: Macmillan, 1972), 193.

2. A limited list of some, not all, scholars engaged in this endeavor: Pierre D. Chantepie de la Saussaye, *Manual of the Science of Religion* (New York: Longmans, Green, 1891); E. E. Evans-Pritchard, *Theories of Primitive Religion* (Oxford: Clarendon, 1965); E. O. James, *Prehistoric Religion* (New York: Barnes and Noble, 1961); Rafael Karsten, *The Origins of Religion* (London: Kegan, Paul, Trench, Trubner, 1935); Andrew Lang, *The Making of Religion* (New York: AMS, 1968); Robert Lowie, *Primitive Religion* (New York: Liveright, 1948).

3. Geo Widengren, "Evolutionism and the Problem of the Origin of Religion," *Ethnos* (1945): 2–3.

4. Classic developments of this theme may be found in Sir James George Frazer, *The Golden Bough* (New York: Macmillan, 1922).

5. See Gerardus van der Leeuw, *Religion in Essence and Manifestation* (New York: Harper and Row, 1963).

6. Wilhelm Schmidt, *The Origin and Growth of Religion* (New York: Cooper Square, 1972).

7. Pierre Teilhard de Chardin, *The Phenomenon of Man* (New York: Harper and Row, 1959).

8. For example, see Lucien Levy-Bruhl, *Primitive Mentality*, Lilian A. Clare, trans. (New York: Macmillan, 1923).

9. Robert Bellah, in *Beyond Belief* (New York: Harper and Row, 1970), paints a developmental picture tracing religion from primitive to archaic to historical to modern but makes it clear he is talking about development from simple to complex institutions, not from bad to good.

10. F. Max Müller, "The Savage," *The Nineteenth Century* 17 (1885): 109–32.

11. David Noss and John Noss, *A History of the World's Religions* (New York: Macmillan, 1990), 379.

12. For a fuller expansion of these themes from a Christian point of view, see Terry C. Muck, *Those Other Religions in Your Neighborhood* (Grand Rapids: Zondervan, 1992).

Chapter 4: Determining the Religious Event

1. Edmund Perry, "What We Study When We Study Religion Instead of the Religions," a paper presented at the International Association of the History of Religions, Helsinki, 1973. "When we study 'religion' we do not study a phantom. We study the eternal world as disclosed in varying modes and content in the several particular religions."

2. This method, when considered the prime method for studying religion, is usually called the history of religions method. See C. J. Bleeker, "Comparing the Religio-Historical and Theological Method," *Numen* 18 (1971): 9–29. Scholars who have developed and championed this approach include Ugo Bianchi, *The History of Religions* (Leiden: Brill, 1975); Mircea Eliade and Joseph Kitagawa, eds., *The History of Religions: Essays in Methodolgy* (Chicago: University of Chicago Press, 1959); Lauri Honko, ed., *Science of Religion: Studies in Methodolgy* (The Hague: Mounton, 1979); Joseph Kitagawa, *The History of Religions* (Atlanta: Scholars, 1987); Arnold Toynbee, *An Historian's Approach to Religion* (Oxford: Oxford University Press, 1979); and Jan De Vries, *Perspectives in the History of Religions* (Berkeley: University of California Press, 1977).

3. The relationship between the Buddha's social ethic and the development of the *sangha*, the community of monks, is an interesting one that needs further scholarly attention. See Sukumar Dutt, *Buddhist Monks and Monasteries of India* (London: George Allen and Unwin, 1962); G. S. P. Misra, *The Age of Vinaya* (New Delhi: Munshiram Manoharlal, 1972); and Charles Prebish, ed., *Buddhist Monastic Discipline* (University Park, Penn.: Pennsylvania State University Press, 1975).

4. See Noor Muhammad, "The Doctrine of Jihad: An Introduction," *Journal of Law and Religion* 3 (1988): 381–97.

5. Groups that don't like the idea of development within their tradition often lie toward the theologically conservative end of the spectrum. For them, the unitive truth of the revelation tends to overshadow the idea of excessive development within the tradition.

6. For example, Wilfred Cantwell Smith, *The Meaning and End of Religion* (New York: Macmillan, 1963).

7. Adherents would say this gives them more than identity; it gives them authority.

8. There are three main encyclopedias that would yield the kind of articles we are talking about in this chapter. James Hastings, ed., *Encyclopedia of Religion and Ethics* (New York: Scribners, 1927); Samuel M. Jackson, ed., *The New Schaff-Herzog Encyclopedia of Religious Knowledge* (Grand Rapids: Baker, 1960–1966); and Mircea Eliade, ed., *The Encyclopedia of Religion* (New York: Macmillan, 1987).

9. See Watson E. Mills, ed., *Directory of Departments and Programs of Religious Studies in North America, Council of Societies for the Study of Religion* (Macon, Ga.: Mercer University Press, 1987), a listing of programs and scholars and their specialities.

10. S. G. F. Brandon, *Time and Mankind* (London: Hutchinson, 1951). Consider also indigenous religions, which tend to be very present oriented, lacking the empha-

sis on future states that characterizes world religions. You might say that their view of time tends to be vertical rather than horizontal.

11. Two scholars who focused on this aspect early in the history of religious studies were Franz Boas and Wilhelm Schmidt, who were part of the German cultural circle school of religious studies. They combined the search for religious origins with a theory regarding how religions spread from culture to culture. Although many of the conclusions of the cultural circle school are no longer given credence, these scholars did focus on questions that today, in different form, are central to religious studies. See Robert H. Lowrie, *The History of Ethnological Theory* (New York: Holt, Rinehart and Winston, 1937).

12. For this reason, the role of the Buddhist monk or *bhikkhu* is quite different from that of the Hindu priest. See Walpola Rahula, *The Heritage of the Bhikkhu* (New York: Grove, 1974), for a discussion of this socially aware role.

13 See Marilyn Ferguson, *The Aquarian Conspiracy: Personal and Social Transformation in the 1980s* (New York: St. Martin's, 1980).

14. John Hick, *An Interpretation of Religion* (New Haven: Yale University Press, 1989), 2.

15. See J. N. D. Anderson, *Christianity and World Religions* (Downers Grove, Ill.: InterVarsity, 1984), and Kenneth Howkins, *The Challenge of Religious Studies* (Downers Grove, Ill.: InterVarsity, 1972), for responsible reactions to the cultural and historical reductionism that occasionally occurs among religious studies scholars.

16. See, for example, Masaharu Anesaki, *History of Japanese Religion* (Rutland, Vt.: C. E. Tuttle, 1963); Joseph Kitagawa, *Religion in Japanese History* (New York: Columbia University Press, 1966); and Sokyo Ono, *Shinto: The Kami Way* (Tokyo: Bridgeway, 1962).

17. See Åke Hulkrantz, "The Phenomenology of Religion: Aims and Methods," *Temenos 6* (1970): 68–88. Joachim Wach, in *Sociology of Religion* (Chicago: University of Chicago Press, 1944), defined phenomenology of religion this way: "The systematic, not historical, study of phenomena like prayer, priesthood, etc.," 1 n. 3.

18. Bleeker ("Comparing the Religio-Historical and Theological Method") does a very helpful job of comparing the history of religions method with theology, sociology of religion, psychology of religion, and phenomenology of religion. He includes a couple of paragraphs on the comparative method of study.

19. See, for example, Andrew Jedrczak, Michael Toomey, and Geoffrey Clements, "The TM-Sidhi Programme, Age, and Brief Tests of Perceptual-Motor Speed and Nonverbal Intelligence," *Journal of Clinical Psychology* 42, 1 (January 1986): 161–64; David Orme-Johnson, Charles Alexander, John Davies, Howard Chandler, Wallace Larimore, "International Peace Project in the Middle East: The Effects of the Maharishi Technology of the Unified Field," *Journal of Conflict Resolution* 32, 4 (December 1988): 776–812; Paul Gelderloos, Phil Goddard, Henry Ahlstrom, Rita Jacoby, "Cognitive Orientation toward Positive Values in Advanced Participants of the TM and TM-Sidhi Program," *Perceptual and Motor Skills* 64 (1987): 1003–12.

Chapter 5: Talking to People about Religion

1. There are numerous books and articles on how to conduct field research, particularly interviews. Here are some places to start: David Bakan, *On Method: Toward a Reconstruction of Psychological Investigation* (San Francisco: Jossey-Bass, 1967); Norman Bradburn and Seymour Sudman, *Improving Interview Method and Questionnaire Design* (San Francisco: Jossey-Bass, 1979); Michael Brenner, Jennifer Brown, and David Canter, eds., *The Research Interview: Uses and Approaches* (London: Academic Press, 1985); Elliot Mishler, *Research Interviewing: Context and Narrative* (Cambridge: Harvard University Press, 1986); and Survey Research Center, *Interviewer's Manual*, rev. ed. (Ann Arbor: University of Michigan Institute for Social Research, 1976).

2. One way to address some of the limitations of pure observation is to become a participant observer, that is, to take part in the event you are observing. Thus, you not only have your observations to rely on, but also your personal experience of the event. Of course, the participant observer profile adds complicating factors to the data collection process. You are not a neutral observer in the first place, and by becoming involved you run the risk of bias in several different ways. See George McCall and J. L. Simmons, eds; *Issues in Participant Observation* (Reading, Mass.: Addison-Wesley, 1969).

3. See Howard Schuman and Stanley Presser, *Questions and Answers in Attitude Surveys: Experiments on Question Form, Wording, and Content* (New York: Academic Press, 1981). On Starbuck, see Eric Sharpe, *Comparative Religion: A History* (LaSalle, Ill.: Open Court, 1986), 106–8. Sharpe says Starbuck can "justifiably be counted among the pioneers of the psychology of religion, if only because he appears to have made the first successful use of the questionnaire method of research." Sharpe then quotes Starbuck on why he developed this method: "The central guiding principle was that the study must deal primarily with the first-hand religious experience of individuals not so much with their theories about religion as with their actual experiences. . . . One must catch at first-hand the feeling of spirituality." E. D. Starbuck, "Religion's Use of Me," in V. T. A. Ferm, ed., *Religion in Transition* (New York: Philosophical Library, 1937), 219.

4. James C. Livingston, *Anatomy of the Sacred: An Introduction to Religion* (New York: Macmillan, 1989), 33–34. See G. W. Allport and B. M. Kramer, "Some Roots of Prejudice," *Journal of Psychology* 22 (1946): 9–39.

5. See notes on handling response bias, in "Survey Research," Earl R. Babbie, *The Practice of Social Research*, 2d ed. (Belmont, Calif.: Wadsworth, 1979).

6. Terry C. Muck, "The Bhikkhu of the Pali Vinaya-Pitaka with an Illustrative Comparison with the Monk of St. Basil's Ascetica," Ph.D. diss., Northwestern University, 1977.

7. It is arguable that the United States's greatest contribution to the field of religious studies is in the area of psychology of religion, that is, uncovering individual religious response and behavior. Both religious studies and the psychology of religion are relatively new disciplines, dating their respective histories to the late nineteenth century. Experimentally, men like G. Stanley Hall (1844–1924), James Leuba (1868–1946), and E. D. Starbuck (1866–1947) broke new ground. And America's greatest psychologist of religion is William James (1842–1910), whose *Varieties of*

Religious Experience (1902) is still considered a classic. Of course, worldwide, religion and psychology are joined in people's minds negatively because of Sigmund Freud (1856–1939) and positively because of Carl Jung (1875–1961).

8. John F. Wilson and W. Royce Clark, *Religion: A Preface*, 2d ed. (Englewood Cliffs, N.J.: Prentice-Hall, 1989), 12.

9. It is interesting to see this growing awareness developing when viewed in the overall history of scientific method. See, for example, John Losee, *A Historical Introduction to the Philosophy of Science* (New York: Oxford University Press, 1972).

10. One of the best discussions of the difficulties and potential in studying the religious life is Frederick J. Streng, *Understanding Religious Life* (Encino, Calif.: Dickenson, 1976), particularly the first chapter.

11. See Terry C. Muck, "The Role of Autobiography in the Comparison of Salvation and Nirvana," *Buddhist–Christian Studies* 12 (1992): 183–89.

Chapter 6: Dissecting the Religious Elements of a Culture

1. For discussions of the limited spread of Hinduism see K. M. Sen, *Hinduism* (New York: Penguin, 1961); Troy Wilson Organ, *Hinduism: Its Historical Development* (Woodbury, N.Y.: Barron's Educational Series, 1974); and R. C. Zaehner, *Hinduism* (New York: Oxford University Press, 1966).

2. See Kenneth K. S. Ch'en, *Buddhism* (Woodbury, N.Y.: Barron's *The Light of Asia Educational Series*, 1968); Edward Conze, *Buddhism: Its Essence and Development* (New York: Harper, 1959); and Peter A. Pardue, *Buddhism* (New York: Macmillan, 1971).

3. In modern times Hinduism has made efforts at missionary work. Starting with the presentations at the World Parliament of Religions at the 1893 Chicago World's Fair, Vivekananda began to teach Hinduism in the United States with modest success. The fourteen Vedanta Societies in major United States cities are the lasting fruits of his labor. Hinduism has begun to spread partly because of attempts to make it more culturally adaptable. The results of these efforts have been "export" Hinduism of various sorts, some close to traditional Indian Hinduism, some not. They include Transcendental Meditation, The International Society for Krishna Consciousness (Hare Krishna), and numerous gurus who have come to America with a made-for-the-West Hindu message.

4. There is no more burning issue in religious studies (and Christian theology) than the relationship of religion to culture. Historically in the study of religions this was also a question of first-rank importance. The earliest scholars of religion tended to be anthropologists who studied entire cultures and religion's role in those cultures. See particularly Michael Banton, ed., *Anthropological Approaches to the Study of Religion* (London: Tavistock, 1968); William Lessa and Evon Vogt, *Reader in Comparative Religion: An Anthropological Approach* (New York: Harper and Row, 1979); Claude Levi-Strauss, *The Savage Mind* (Chicago: University of Chicago Press, 1966); Bronislaw Malinowski, *Magic, Science and Religion* (Garden City, N.Y.: Doubleday, 1948); and Paul Radin, *Primitive Religion* (New York: Dover, 1937). Modern schol-

ars of religion and culture do not ask the same questions that these anthropologists did. But much of their work is still useful.

5. This is meant to be a happy analogy. All analogies have limits, and this one does too. But I trust the point is helpful.

6. See my two books on the subject of religious pluralism in America, *Alien Gods on American Turf* (Wheaton, Ill.: Victor, 1990) and *Those Other Religions in Your Neighborhood* (Grand Rapids: Zondervan, 1992).

7. See Robert Bellah, *Beyond Belief* (New York: Harper and Row, 1970).

8. Two books by Jack Weatherford discuss the influences of Native American religions on American culture: *Indian Givers: How the Indians of the Americas Transformed the World* (New York: Crown, 1988), and *Native Roots: How the Indians Enriched America* (New York: Crown, 1991).

9. Several things can happen when religions meet one another in a culture. One may supplant the other. They may combine. There may be mutual influence (syncretism). All of these processes have been thoroughly studied by religious studies scholars. Sometimes religions attempt to place themselves above the fray of the religion-culture clash through some form of separation. Consider a sampling of sociology of religion texts to get a sense for where this type of study leads: Emile Durkheim, *The Elementary Forms of the Religious Life* (New York: Macmillan, 1915); Claude Levi-Strauss, *The Savage Mind* (Chicago: University of Chicago Press, 1966); Roland Robertson, ed., *Sociology of Religion* (Baltimore: Penguin, 1969); Louis Schneider, *Religion, Culture and Society: A Reader in the Sociology of Religion* (New York: John Wiley, 1964). Th. P. van Baaren and H. J. W. Drijvers, eds., *Religion, Culture, and Methodology* (The Hague: Mouton, 1973); Joachim Wach, *Sociology of Religion* (Chicago: University of Chicago Press, 1944); Max Weber, *The Sociology of Religion* (Boston: Beacon, 1963).

10. Several good books have been written on how to analyze a community. See Roland Leslie Warren, *Studying Your Community* (New York: Free Press, 1965); Stephen Bochner, ed., *Cultures in Contact: Studies in Cross-Cultural Interaction* (Oxford: Pergamon, 1982); and Joe Holland and Peter Henriot, *Social Analysis: Linking Faith and Justice* (Maryknoll, N.Y.: Orbis, 1983). Of course, the most famous example of this kind of community analysis is the one started by Robert and Helen Lynd in 1929 on Muncie, Indiana. They published the results of their first analysis, *Middletown* (New York: Harcourt, Brace and Co., 1929) and then updated their study ten years later in *Middletown in Transition: A Study in Cultural Conflicts* (New York: Harcourt, Brace and Co., 1937). They analyzed Muncie's religious make-up in Section 5, "Engaging in Religious Practices." Others have since updated their study even further.

11. Mercer Town Meeting, Mercer, Wisconsin, July 25, 1991.

Chapter 7: Comparing and Contrasting Religious Traditions

1. A religion of India traced back to a sixth century B.C.E. teacher, Vardhamana, also known as Mahavira (Great Hero).

2. Luther complained that merited salvation was the net effect of the church's selling of indulgences in the sixteenth century; there are hints of earned salvation in several modern theologies.

3. See Eric Sharpe, *Comparative Religion: A History* (LaSalle, Ill.: Open Court, 1986).

4. William Paden in *Religious Worlds: The Comparative Study of Religion* (Boston: Beacon, 1988) discusses thoroughly this history, as does Sharpe in *Comparative Religion*. The initial scholars of this approach included F. Max Müller, E. B. Tylor, and R. R. Marett. See also Louis Henry Jordan, *Comparative Religion: Its Genesis and Growth* (Edinburgh: T & T Clark, 1905), and A. C. Bouquet, *Comparative Religion*, 7th ed. (Baltimore: Penguin, 1967).

5. Gerardus van der Leeuw, *Religion in Essence and Manifestation* (New York: Harper and Row, 1963), and Mircea Eliade, *Patterns in Comparative Religion* (New York: World, 1963). See also Sir James George Frazer, *The Golden Bough* (New York: Macmillan, 1922).

6. An excellent comparative study on prayer was done by Friedrich Heiler, *Prayer: A Study in the History and Psychology of Religion*, Samuel McComb, trans. (London: Oxford University Press, 1932).

7. Robert Bellah, *Beyond Belief* (New York: Harper and Row, 1970,) 20–48.

8. See Paden, *Religious Worlds*, 23, quoting from Alexander Ross, *Pansebeia or a View of All the Religions of the World*, 6th ed. (London: Gillyflower and Freeman, 1696), 381.

9. James Freeman Clarke, *Ten Great Religions* (Boston: Houghton, Mifflin, 1893).

10. Laurette Sejourne, *Burning Water: Thought and Religion in Ancient Mexico* (Berkeley, Calif.: Shambhala, 1976).

11. F. Max Müller, *Introduction to the Science of Religion* (London: Longmans, Green, 1873), 16.

12. For an excellent summary of the many different ways comparison is done in religious studies today, see Frank Whaling, ed., *Contemporary Approaches to the Study of Religion* (Berlin: Mouton, 1983), 1:165–295.

13. The comparison I'm citing here is one done successfully by one of my students, Karen Greif, at Austin Presbyterian Theological Seminary in 1990.

14. See, for example, T. W. Rhys Davids, *Buddhist India* (Freeport, N.Y.: Books for Libraries, 1972, repr. of 1903 ed.).

15. Perhaps the first religious historian to give this element its due was Johann Gottfried Herder (1744–1803). See Robert T. Clark's study of Herder, *Herder: His Life and Thought* (Berkeley: University of California Press, 1955).

16. (New York: Macmillan, 1930).

17. See Roger Keller, *Reformed Christians and Mormon Christians* (Pryor Pettengill, 1986).

Chapter 8: The Questions of Truth, Value, and Effectiveness

1. For diverse examples of philosophical approaches to the question of truth, read scholars like Robert Baird, *Category Formation in the History of Religions* (The

Hague: Mouton, 1971); S. G. F. Brandon, *Time and Mankind* (London: Hutchinson, 1951); Samuel Coleridge, *Confessions of an Inquiring Spirit* (Menston, England: Scolar, 1971); David Hume, *Dialogues Concerning Natural Religion* (London: Thomas Nelson, 1947); Leszek Kolakowski, *Religion, If There Is No God* (New York: Oxford University Press, 1982); Gotthold Lessing, *Theological Writings* (Stanford: Stanford University Press, 1956); Hajime Nakamura, *Parallel Developments: A Comparative History of Ideas* (Tokyo: Kodansha, 1975); Schubert Ogden, "Problems in the Case for a Pluralistic Theology of Religions," *The Journal of Religion* 68 (October 1988): 493–507; Paul Ricoeur, *History and Truth* (Evanston, Ill.: Northwestern University Press, 1965); and Donald Wiebe, *Religion and Truth* (The Hague: Mouton, 1981).

2. Consider writings by Peter Berger, *The Sacred Canopy* (Garden City, N.Y.: Doubleday, 1967); Roland Robertson, ed., *Sociology of Religion* (Baltimore: Penguin, 1969); Herbert Spencer, *Principles of Sociology* (London: Macmillan, 1969); Max Weber, *The Sociology of Religion* (Boston: Beacon, 1963); B. R. Wilson, *Religion in Secular Society* (Harmondsworth: Penguin, 1969); and J. M. Yinger, *The Scientific Study of Religion* (New York: Macmillan, 1970).

3. In addition to Freud, other psychologists of religion to consider include Gordon Allport, *The Individual and His Religion* (New York: Macmillan, 1961); W. H. Clark, *The Psychology of Religion* (New York: Macmillan, 1958); Erich Fromm, *The Dogma of Christ* (Garden City, N.Y.: Doubleday, 1963); Carl Gustav Jung, *Modern Man in Search of a Soul* (New York: Harcourt, Brace, 1933); J. B. Pratt, *The Psychology of Religious Belief* (New York: Macmillan, 1907); and Paul Pruyser, *A Dynamic Psychology of Religion* (New York: Harper and Row, 1968).

4. Theologians represent as wide a spectrum in their approaches to the question of truth as do philosophers, sociologists, and psychologists. Consider as examples, John B. Cobb, Jr., *Christ in a Pluralistic Age* (Philadelphia: Westminster, 1975); Ludwig Feuerbach, *The Essence of Christianity* (New York: Harper, 1957); Hans Küng, "What Is True Religion?" in *Toward a Universal Theology of Religion*, Leonard Swidler, ed. (Maryknoll, N.Y.: Orbis, 1987); Leon Morris, *The Abolition of Religion* (Downers Grove, Ill.: InterVarsity, 1964); Paul Tillich, "Christian Principles of Judging Non-Christian Religions," in *Christianity and the Encounter of the World Religions* (New York: Columbia University Press, 1963); Ernst Troeltsch, *The Absoluteness of Christianity and the History of Religions* (Richmond, Va.: John Knox, 1971); and Alfred North Whitehead, *Religion in the Making* (New York: Macmillan, 1926).

5. See Mortimer Adler, *Truth in Religion* (New York: Macmillan, 1990), for a clear exposition of the classical approach. For one modern development of this position see Ludwig Wittgenstein, *Tractatus Logico-Philosophicus*, D. F. Pears and B. F. McGuinness, trans., rev. ed. (London: Routledge and Kegan Paul, 1974).

6. Augustine, *Of True Religion* (Chicago: Regnery, 1959).

7. Immanuel Kant, *Critique of Pure Reason*, Norman Kemp Smith, trans. (New York: St. Martin's, 1968).

8. Friedrich Schleiermacher, *The Christian Faith* (Edinburgh: T & T Clark, 1989).

9. Søren Kierkegaard, "Of the Difference between a Genius and an Apostle," in *The Present Age* (New York: Harper and Row, 1962), cited in David Lochhead, "Christian Upaya: Variations on a Theme by Søren Kierkegaard," an unpublished paper whose argument helped me a great deal in this brief summary.

10. The following paragraphs are based on Wilfred Cantwell Smith's arguments from "Can Religions Be True or False?" in *Questions of Religious Truth* (New York: Scribner, 1967), "A Human View of Truth," in *Truth and Dialogue: The Relationship between World Religions,* John Hick, ed. (London: Sheldon, 1974), and "Comparative Religion: Whither and Why?" in *Religious Diversity: Essays* (New York: Harper and Row, 1976).

11. Frederick Streng, "Truth," in *The Encyclopedia of Religion,* Mircea Eliade, ed. (New York: Macmillan, 1987). See also Streng's discussion of religious truth in *Understanding Religious Life* (Encino, Calif.: Dickenson, 1976).

12. Roger Nicole, "The Biblical Concept of Truth," in *Scripture and Truth,* D. A. Carson and John D. Woodbridge, eds. (Grand Rapids: Baker, 1992). See also, Hendrick Kraemer, "Continuity or Discontinuity," in *Authority of the Faith* (London: Oxford University Press, 1939).

13. Dayananda Sarasvati, *Dayananda-Shastrarth-Sangraha* (Bombay: Sonipat, 1969), 35. See also J. T. F. Jordens, *Dayananda Sarasvati: His Life and Ideas* (Dehli: Oxford University Press, 1978).

14. Rodney Stark, "How New Religions Succeed: A Theoretical Model," in *The Future of New Religious Movements,* David Bromley and Phillip Hammond, eds. (Macon, Ga.: Mercer University Press, 1987), 11–29.

15. John Hick, *An Interpretation of Religion* (New Haven: Yale University Press, 1989). See also Hick's "Grading Religions," *Religious Studies* 17 (1981): 45–67, and "The Outcome," in *Truth and Dialogue,* 140–55. Quote is from *Truth and Dialogue,* 155.

16. Wolfhart Pannenberg, "The Nature of a Theological Statement," *Zygon* (1972): 6–19; "What Is Truth?" in *Basic Questions in Theology,* vol. 2, George H. Kehm, trans. (Philadelphia: Fortress, 1971), 1–27.

17. See Raimundo Panikkar, "The Category of Growth in Comparative Religions," *Harvard Theological Review* 66 (1973): 113–40; quote is from p. 135.

Index

157